ELÄMÄN ULAPALLA, ANNI AHOLA kertoo

Translated from Finnish by Päivi Torkki
Edited by David J. Granlund, Ph.D.

ON THE HIGH SEAS OF LIFE

By Anni Ahola

i

ISBN 978-0-615-44010-1

Cover design by Alan McCoy

I hope you will enjoy reading Amalia's stories.

David J Granlund

Table of Contents

INTRODUCTION

Amalia (Ylen) Kytölä, my grandmother, was born 26 June 1889 in Tuusula just north of Helsinki, Finland. Shortly after her mother's death 4 March 1902, her father immigrated to the United States. A year later Amalia traveled, unescorted at the age of 14, to join her father. She had an adventuresome life living and working in Minnesota before marrying and homesteading in the wilds of northern Minnesota. It had to be a real adjustment to come from Finland where she had enjoyed the conveniences of electricity, telephone and indoor plumbing and then to live for decades in northern Minnesota before these conveniences became available to the homesteading Finns in Carlton County.

Her education began in Finland where she completed 3 years of high school. She continued her education in Minnesota where she attended night classes and short courses at the University of Minnesota for an additional 5 years. Along with starting a family and raising 11 children in the wilderness, she worked side by side with her husband in lumber camps as well as on their homestead. For 10 years she served as her township's treasurer. She was the first woman in Minnesota to serve on the Community Soil Conservation Committee. Not surprisingly, she was an avid gardener.

Amalia loved to read and to write. She wrote under the pen name Anni Ahola. She composed a series of 10 stories for the Finnish newspaper "Päivälehti" in 1942 as well as several other news articles and commentaries. The anthology that follows here is a fictionalized autobiography of this amazing woman. There were 52 episodes that appeared in "Keskilännen Sanomat" (KS) between June 1954 and January 1955. I have preserved the episodes of "Elämän Ulalpalla, Anni Ahola kertoo" in their content as they appeared in the original Finnish text. In addition to the translation of the 52 episodes, I have integrated the early series of ten stories translated from Päivälehti into the second series while attempting to maintain her writing style and characteristic delivery.

There are many people to thank for bringing this work to print. My cousin Gloria gave me copies of 50 of the original KS newspaper stories. Her mother had rescued those copies of the old newspapers from the house after Amalia died 1 Feb 1964 and saved them for years. Through the diligent efforts of Päivi Torkki, a professional translator who lives in a town very close to Tuusula (where Amalia was born), these wonderful stories in Finnish can now be enjoyed by those of us that have either forgotten our Finnish or never mastered the Finnish language. Päivi alerted me that there were some obvious gaps in the story flow as she developed the translation. Through the assistance of Sara Wakefield with The Immigration History Research Center, College of Liberal Arts, Elmer L. Anderson Library at the University of Minnesota, the two missing KS episodes were found and added to complete the collection. The stories are fascinating for their historic perspective of a woman's life in northern Minnesota during that time period. I found them to be addicting and could hardly wait for the next episode. It was a rare opportunity for me to get to know my grandmother, Amalia, in her own words and thoughts. This has been a project of great joy and satisfaction. I hope you too will enjoy Grandmother Amalia Kytölä's stories, "On the High Seas of Life by Anni Ahola".

I am admittedly biased in my opinion of the worth of this body of work. Therefore, you will find a translated independent tribute in the appendix. It appeared in KS 7 February 1955 at the conclusion of the series and it was written by A. W. Havela, president of the KS publishing company.

David J. Granlund, Ph.D.

PART I: CHILDHOOD, EPISODES 1-6

Episode 1, 29 Jun 1954

Tuol' Pohjanlahden rannalla	There on the shores of the Gulf of Bothnia
viheriäisellä nurmella	in the green grass
on kotini vaikk' matala	is my home, though lowly
se ompi mulle kultala	for me it is a golden place

So sang Anni Ahola, sitting by herself, knitting a mitten from soft gray wool, by a warm stove, on a cold December night. She had already passed the half-century mark, but she still had a singing voice. She still remembered all old familiar Finnish songs. They remained fresh in her mind though she had left her country of birth as a child. How else could the Finnish Proverb "What you learn young, you master well when you're older" be true.

Repeating the last verse, Anni saw that the children Elizabeth, Jaakko and Antti were running, as if competing with each other, from the yard towards the door -they were the youngest Ahola children -the last still at home, of a total of twelve children. "Mother, all evening chores are done, and now it is so, Mother, that we heard your singing and it reminded us of a promise you once made to us", said Elizabeth, "do you remember, Mother dear". "Why of course I do remember", said the mistress of Ahola. "I promised to tell you about my childhood and my country of birth, Finland." "Yes that's it", continued Elizabeth, "and we won't settle just with you telling us about your childhood, we want to hear everything about your

2

life, all up to and until these very days. Tell us about your school days, and your youth-time loves, for you must have had many of them in your life. Tell us about all the dreams, hopes and disappointments of your youth, and the thoughts of your older days." "However we don't want to wear you out so that you must tell us a lot at a time, rather tell us a little every night", asked Jaakko. "The long winter nights are ahead of us, and Father is not at home, so what better way to spend the nights, and besides where could we possibly go from behind these big snow drifts", pondered Antti.

The mistress of Ahola smiled a crafty smile, asking, how soon would you then have me start telling my story? - Right this very moment, said three mouths at the same time -and they sat down around the stove to see whether Mother really would start, and so did the mistress Anni Ahola commence.

I reckon you would like to hear about life in Finland. I know very little about the country life, because I only lived in the countryside for two summers and then only for a couple of weeks, so my memories of many things are hazy.

My earliest childhood years are not all that clear in my memories, but I may be able to tell a little bit from here and there. My Father was only twenty-one years old when I was born, my Mother was much older. My home was quite near the railroad, with only a wide gravel road and the high bank of the railroad between them. In summertime the railroad banks were a wonderful field of flowers. In July, red strawberries grew there, and Father sang to me:

Makeoita mansikoita   Sweet
                                       strawberries

syödä saadaan kohta,	We may soon eat
kun toinen puoli on punainen	When one cheek is red
ja toinenkin jo hohtaa.	And the other glows too.

My Mother was deeply religious, and I can still remember many of the hymns she used to sing. They are among my earliest childhood memories. She taught me to sing:

Mä silmät luon ylös taivaaseen	I cast my eyes towards the Heaven
ja käten yhtehen liitän	and put my hands together
Sua Herra ystävä lapsien	You, Lord, friend of children
mä sydämestäni kiitän.	I thank from my heart.

A large brick factory was located near our house. It employed a lot of unmarried men who were quartered in the nearby houses. We had no boarders, but mother baked, sewed and knitted for them. Almost everyday Mother would pull deliciously smelling round rye bread or other types of bread loaves out of the large brick oven. It is difficult to describe that oven, it resembled the open-fire ovens here, but it was wide and low inside. It was wood fired, and embers and ashes were carefully swept out with fir-branch broom. Then bread was placed in the oven, to bake over the hot bricks, and the hatch

4

closed tightly.

I already mentioned that my mother used to sew for the workers. Their underclothes were made from white cotton, and how they managed to stay so white is beyond my comprehension. The way they were laundered must have helped. The work shirts, which Mother also sewed by the dozens, were made from a blue fabric, and the workers would come and pick them up as soon as mother had some finished.

I remember one of the workers especially well. He regularly dropped by for some bread, and each time he would talk to me. He was very short, a small man and once I went and stood next to him, put my hand on his shoulder and said, we are the two little ones. Afterwards I got teased so much for this that it is no wonder I remember it so clearly, though I was only four years old.

Mother was always busy at her chores. She sewed work shirts for the workers of the brick factory. Many of them were single men who cooked their own meals. Mother would bake for them, and almost every day, a delicious smell of fresh bread would waft from room to room. Often Father would pick me up to sit on his knee while Mother was busy baking, and he would sing:

Lapsi makaa kehdossa	The child is sleeping in her cot
ja oma Isä tuutii	with her own Father a-rocking her
Lapsen Äiti tuvassa	The child's Mother is in the

uuniansa luutii

kitchen
sweeping the
oven with a
broom

On the south side of the house there grew a large silver birch whih large, hanging branches that touched the pillars of the verandah. Under this birch Mother grew wormwood from which she picked and dried for the winters. Mother believed that wormwood tea was the best medicine for childrens' stomach ailments. Sometimes, if I complained of a stomach ache, she brought me a cup of steaming wormwood tea. Il was biller to drink even with sugar, but when Mother poured it in a pretty little cup my Godfather had brought me as a present from Helsinki, why then the wormwood tea was not so bitter after all. I admired the cup and saucer; they had broad green and golden stripes. They were used only rarely. Once I asked my father, what does the word "godparent" mean? He said that a godparent is a person who witnesses a child's christening and is responsible for the upbringing of this child in case the child becomes orphaned.   My Godfather, Mr. Lönroos, was married to my Father's sister, Aunt Linda, and they had carried me to the church to be christened. My name certainly was not made overly long, because I was named simply Anni.

Once I asked my Father, where did they get me from, and he answered gravely that they had found me in "Aalloppi". Now, that "Aalloppi", it was a curious place. It was really a river, across which a high railroad bridge had been built, with sort of concrete walkways on both sides underneath it. On laundry days, women

6

would take large basins full of washed clothes there. The clothes were rinsed in the "Aalloppi", then hoisted wet on tall benches, then beaten flat and smooth with a planed wood staff, one end of which had been shaped to fit well in one's hand. The entire bridge would echo with sound, when several women were simultaneously rinsing and beating, and rinsing and beating their clothes.

This process made the clothes practically shine with whiteness. I had fun watching, and sometimes I went so close that water would splash over me. And when a train happened to cross the bridge, now that was great fun, what with such loud hum and clanging that one could not hear another speak, not even thunder could cause such an incredible rumble.

Once, my Father took me with him to the city where my Godfather Lönroos lived. He lived with his wife, Aunt Linda (my Father's sister). I do not remember the trip that clearly, as I was only four years old. Neither do I remember how we got up into the tall building in which they lived. When I looked out of the window and downwards, people on the street looked as if they were just dwarves. Uncle and Aunt had tastefully decorated rooms. One room had a door that opened to the roof where there was a garden out of a fairytale, with flowers of many colors. A tall fence was built around this roof garden, and benches were put here and there, between the flower beds.

I did not ask anyone anything, I simply watched, and nobody did seem to notice me. I thought to myself that in a big city little girls are not paid any attention at all, but it did not bother me in the least. I was happy making my own observations. I returned to the room from which I had entered the roof garden, and sat on a sofa by the window. Now I heard voices somewhere nearby, in another room. It was Uncle Lönroos, speaking in a restrained, sad voice. I heard fragments of sentences. "Must go to America" who had to go? Why? --Then I heard Aunt Linda say, "Yes Antoni, it is decided, then. The Polaris will make her next trip at a time most convenient for you, next month. I promise that all preparations for the trip will be completed by then. Aleksi has already put the money in a bank in your name, and you may withdraw it whenever you want."

"Is everything over, oh Linda, is my love worth nothing to you? Don't you remember that you promised to forget Aleksi when you got engaged to me, even though I was poor? It must be just that you find Aleksi's money and high standing so appealing."

(To be continued)

Episode 2, 2 Jul 1954

"Oh Antoni, don't talk like that, don't you remember that even as a child I loved Aleksi, and he loved me, though he could not tell his parents because I was just a poor factory worker's daughter. And that is why he sent me here, in the city, to be educated and to learn the manners of the better people. And when I nearly was a "Mademoiselle", you appeared and charmed me for a while, and so I agreed to marry you, thinking I could never learn enough to become equal with Aleksi. Do you remember how we read a letter from Aleksi together, right after our wedding? Did he not write how he could never forget me, but because I was deceitful

8

and took you Antoni, so perhaps he would also find someone to be his partner in life.

That's how it was back then, Antoni, but now he is free because his wife died last autumn, and now he wants what is his, so you Antoni have but one road. When you go to America, you can live care-free on the money that Aleksi has invested for you, and besides you will do me a good deed by stepping out of the way of my happiness.

Had I fallen asleep and had a nightmare, or was I truly awake? -- Is my kind Uncle Lönroos to go away, to America? No, no, I felt like crying. My little heart was thumping hard. I realized that something was completely wrong, but could not understand what it was: after all, here were Uncle Lönroos and Aunt Linda, looking so happy in their beautiful home. Aunt had just thrown a birthday party. Why, even her dress had been of beautiful red silk. --I was still crying -- and from afar I could hear music, and lyrics:

Miksi itket,	Why are you crying
tyttöni pieni?	my little girl?
Mikä on sun surusi?	What is your sorrow?
Kerro se mulle,	Tell it to me,
ystävä pieni.	little friend.

All that I had seen and heard whirled around in my thoughts, and it was not until a couple of years later that I would hear much more about what I could not comprehend now. -- In time my visit ended, and Father came to take me home. Aunt furnished me with all sorts of goodies to give to Mother back at

9

home. We were at the door, leaving, when Aunt said: wait just a little, so I can give you a couple of wedges of "arguusi" in a bag. I suppose it was 2 (water melon).

So we said good-bye and promised to give Mother their greetings. We walked up one street and down another, finally arriving at the Esplanadi. But oh grief, the bottom of the paper bag I was carrying fell off, and the "arguusi" wedges fell to the pavement. Their juice had soaked the bottom of the bag, and I had to leave those delicacies there, to my great misery. That's all I remember of the return trip.

Soon after these events we moved to the city, and a whole new world opened in front of me, though city life back then was at its earliest stages, in comparison with life today. -- For example, horses were still used to pull trams. Pairs of horses pulled the trams, and at the end of a long line were the stables where a fresh team would replace the exhausted. After several requests my Father took me to the very end of the long Fredrikinkatu, so that I could see the stables and changing of horses. Everything was so different in the city, and sometimes I noticed that Father was also thinking about the life in the countryside, as one night he took me on knee and started to sing:

Tarkka talon haltia,	A careful master of the house
hän pitää vaarin ajasta	keeps on top of times
Kylmälläkin pakkasella	Even in the coldest weather
hän menee ulos majasta.	he will go out of the house.

Hakoja hakataan,	Branches are chopped
kuusia karsitaan	Fir trees are cut
Kaikkia mitä talossa tarvitaan.	All things required in the house.

But then he continued:

Mutta laiska renki lontti	But the farmhand, that lazy sod
Makas aamulla kahdeksaan.	slept until eight in the morning.
Hän hakee sukkaa, saapastansa	He searches for his socks, boots
Löytää kunkin paikastansa	finding each in the spot
Mink' on illalla viskannu	where he tossed them last night
Penkin alle paiskannu ja	under the bench, and
aamulla ne märkänä	in the morning all wet
sieltä löytää.	he finds them there.

This amused me, but it also reminded me that I should also put my socks up to dry, and I slid down from Father's knee to see to it. The place I put my socks must have been too hot because Mother went and moved them to another place, saying "Wool burns where butter melts".

Our new home in town was not a single house,

but a group of houses, with two spacious shop stores at the front and living quarters at the back. On the other side of the yard there was a large canteen and the janitor's apartment. The yard was a large garden with a couple of pear trees, four apple trees and a weeping willow, a couple of gooseberry and currant bushes, and a row of lilac bushes. Under these trees Mother placed a table and some chairs. On summer evenings, we would often sit there, having tea with our neighbors, but often by ourselves. In springtime, the sweet perfume of the apple blossoms would float in through the open windows.

Once it occurred to me to pick some apple blossoms. Looking out of the window Mother saw what I was up to. In the blink of an eye she came rushing to me. She gave me a proper spanking and talking-to, explaining: how shall we get apples for the winter, if the blossoms are torn off. I stayed there for a moment, crying for my own stupidity. Mother had finished scolding me and vanished. From somewhere, through an open window, there was singing:

Miksi itket lapsi kulta,	Why are you crying, dear child,
miksi olet rauhaton,	why are you restless,
Joko elon myrskyt sulta	have the storms of life already
rikkonut sun rauhas	disturbed your piece of mind
Nuori viel' on elämäsi	Your life is still young
runneltavaksi surujen	to be damaged

by sorrows

I had no time to listen for more, because that big fat sheep came charging at me, but I made it to the door and managed to open it before the sheep had time to give me a push. The janitor and his old wife lived in one of the buildings in the backyard. It was their job to keep the yard, the garden and our section of the street tidy. For this purpose they had a horse and a two-wheeled cart. All work, except for the street sweeping, had to be done at night.

The janitor had stables at the back of the yard. There he kept a horse, and this big ewe which for some unknown reason was mad at children. She could give you a push like a ram, and she would charge at you slyly, when one did not realize that she had been let out again. If I unwittingly went to the yard then, I got quite a bump if I didn't make it to the door before she caught up with me. Finally I learned to be cautious, so that when I was coming home from somewhere, I would open the gate just a little to see if the sheep was out in the yard, and if she was, I would shut the gate and go in from the front, through the shop. I was not actually allowed to do that, but when I explained to my father why I did it, he did not scold me. Once when I had used that entrance several times, Father told me: "Remember from now on to use only the door from the yard." I obeyed, and the sheep had vanished. Now I was again able to play freely in the yard.

The apple trees bore large crops. Mother would collect apples in boxes, for storage in the cellar, and she also sliced up and dried plenty of apples.

Several years later I walked past my old home.

The garden had gone, and in its place stood a large building built of stone. It was the janitor's job to keep the yard, garden and our section of the street tidy. The street was laid of small stones up to the edge of the pavement, and in the summertime grass would push through between the stones, and it had to be pulled out. I often saw the janitor's wife kneeling by the pavement, pulling out grass with a small knife, but it was more fun watching her sweep the yard, because when she made right-to-left sweeping motions with the broom, her tongue seemed to travel in pace with the broom.

(To be continued)

Episode 3, 9 July 1954

On one rainy day it was quiet in the store. I crept in but Father noticed me instantly. He said, "Now you may play here for a while, if you don't disturb anything". Oh, what joy, I thought, this is going to be fun. Father was sitting behind the counter, apparently immersed in book keeping. I climbed into a big wooden box which had been left high on the stairs. I don't know how I moved about inside the box, but it fell down the stairs, taking me with it. Nails sticking out from the sides of the box stabbed me in the head. I woke up in my bed in my room, my head wrapped in bandages. Uncle Lönroos was sitting on a chair beside me. He looked so sad, and I asked what had happened to me. He told me he had happened to step into the store at the very moment I had fallen down. He had picked me up and called the doctor. When he finished the story, he took a shiny one-mark

14

coin from his pocket, gave it to me, said his good-byes and left. It was fun to receive a mark, as I had not had the chance to add to my "bank account" in a while. My Father had taught me to read as soon as I turned four. I can not remember what my ABC book looked like, but I do remember that a big rooster was pictured in the back leaf. When my reading exercises went particularly well, a five- or a ten-penny coin would mysteriously appear right next to the picture of the rooster, and I would find it the next morning while I was leafing through my ABC book. Without exception, every coin would go straight into my piggy bank. I remember being very careful when it came to money.

Father had given me money for reading the ABC book, and I would save every penny, but now Father said I would soon be of school age, so the ABC book was left unread, though I did not start school that autumn. A lot of older pupils arrived from the countryside to the schools in town. Many pupils lived in boarding houses, but some wanted to find families with whom they could stay during their school terms.

Mother took a student organist to live with us. He would practice his lessons on our piano. His name was Urho Himanko. One night he asked my Father whether he would like him to teach me the basics of piano playing. My Father accepted happily his kind offer, and so my piano lessons started. I don't remember how many lessons I had, or how much time they took, but finally, to my Father's joy and my teacher's pride I was able to play and sing:

Erämaata, erämaata   In wilderness,
                            wilderness

läpi kulkeissain	where I went a-wandering
Kuulen puhuttavan,	I heard it said
todeks' sanottavan	said as a truth
Että kerran, että kerran	that one day, one day
pääsen kotihin.	I will reach my home

"Run here quickly, Anni", shouted Mother on a beautiful cold autumn day. Why on earth is such a rush necessary, I wondered to myself while running to my mother. She started to dress me up in a good dress and said that Aunt Linda had called for us to come to the harbor, to say good-bye to Uncle Lönroos who was leaving for America.

We rushed to the harbor and from far away I could see the big letters on the side of the ship. Having studied them for a while I realized that she was the "Polaris". Then I remembered where I had heard that name before, why, this very summer, when I was visiting Uncle and Aunt Lönroos. I remembered Aunt Linda saying that the ship would sail in a month's time, but it was late autumn now. Unavoidable obstacles must have cropped up to delay Uncle's departure.

There were plenty of friends and relatives of Uncle Lönroos at the harbor. Uncle said good-bye to everyone, and when my turn came, he lifted me high up in the air, then put me down gently and whispered, "Good-bye, dear child". I waited, excited, for the ship to cast off and start to distance herself from the slip, and I saw that even though Uncle was supposed to travel alone, there was another person standing next to Uncle. I looked more closely and realized it was Aunt Linda, standing right next to Uncle. I was happy, thinking that Aunt had decided to go with Uncle after all. I was thrilled, watching the ship, thinking she would surely cast off now, but no. Aboard the ship, Aunt Linda tied a pretty bouquet to Uncle's breast, then gave him a quick kiss on the cheek and walked quickly down to the slip. Years later, thinking about that event, it occurred to me that it was "a Judas kiss", though my young brain could not comprehend what really had happened, and -- but so as not to rush ahead of the story, I shall come back to this matter later and tell what I learned of Uncle Lönroos's trip to America. The ship sailed off to the open seas, and we rushed home. Mother had tears in her eyes as she took me by the hand, and I felt as if short of breath even when were home again. All I could think about was my Uncle, and I remembered a song that would be perfect for him:

Yksinäin, yksinäin	Alone, alone
täytyy pois mun rientää näin,	must I hasten away now
Silmän peittää kyynel karvas,	Bitter tears flow from my eyes
Kauas jäi mun maani armas,	Far behind is left my dear country
Kauas kallis synnyinmaa.	far behind lies my beloved country of birth

In my mind I traveled with Uncle to the foreign land, sure that once in America, Uncle would remember these verses:

Pohjolain, pohjolain,	My northern country, my

	northern country
Siel ol' hauska vaeltain.	it was good to go a-wandering there.
Vaan tääl' ei äidinkieli kaiu.	But here mother tongue is not heard
Huuliltain ei laulut vaiu.	My lips will not forget songs
Kaukana on äidinkiel.	Far away is mother tongue.

One sunny Sunday Father decided that we would go to "Korkeasaari" to see all the animals. "Korkeasaari" is what is here called a "zoo". Visitors were taken there by boat, so now I, too, would experience what it was like to be on board a boat, though the trip did not take all that many minutes. When we got there and were observing all the various animals, I had to wonder, how they possibly manage to feed them all. In one place a large and strong steel cage had been built on the bank of the island. From the top of the hill one could easily look down into the cage and see its inhabitants, which were two polar bears. In addition to us, there were lots of people watching them. A very dignified looking lady was standing there, holding a little lapdog in her arms. The dog had a tasteful little "overcoat" wrapped on his back, decorated with tiny bells. I don't know whether the lady got nervous, or whether the dog moved too suddenly, because it slipped down from the lady's arms, fell down into the cage, and instantly a polar bear grabbed it into its mouth, overcoat and bells and all. The lady started to cry wildly, and Father took

18

me by the hand and walked me off, to find more amusing sights to see. During the return trip I fell asleep in Father's arms, and when I woke up I was sorry to think I might have missed seeing anything important.

The following Sunday Mother asked whether I would like to go with them to the church. It was the "St. Nicholas church", the largest and most beautiful in Helsinki (its current name is the Lutheran Cathedral). A long staircase with high steps made my knees tired, but when we entered the church, it was so solemn to hear the gentle organ music. I wondered to myself whether our student organist Urho Himanko was allowed to play that organ during weekdays, for practice. He must be very proud when he can return to his home town a fully learned organist. My thoughts went a-wondering, and finally they settled on a story of two farm owners from Savo who came to the city to run some errands and would stay in town over the weekend.

(To be continued)

Episode 4, 13 Jul 1954

The two farmers happened to walk past the church just when somebody was playing the organ. They wondered about the sound. One farmer decided to go in and told the other to wait. Soon he came out and said to the waiting man, "Jaakko, come and see, a machine is singing". Together they went inside, and soon the second man said, "By all things in Heaven, but if that isn't a grand sound."

The winter started unexpectedly harsh and cold already before Christmas, and the Gulf of Finland froze and was covered in thick ice unusually early. The newspapers announced that the Finnish ice breaker "Murtaja" would arrive to keep the waterways open for ships. Father promised to take me with him to witness her arrival. It was such a majestic sight that one can never forget it. The ice was like cheese, it crumbled and moved aside, out of the way of that power; the crackling and whooshing was so loud that it was impossible to hear what Father was saying.

Several other interesting events occurred during those days."Andrea's trip to the North Pole" kept everyone talking. He decided to make the trip by balloon, and to beef up the trip fund, small, red, round badges with Andrea's picture and a description of the trip were sold all over town. The badge had a ribbon so that it could be tied to one's breast, and it cost a mark. Father bought me a badge and I have kept it for all these years. One could not see anyone without a badge, so enthusiastic was everyone about this trip. I believe it happened in 1894, and in those days there were no airplanes yet. A couple of years ago we read in the newspaper that the remains of this very same Andrea, along with his notes, had been found at the North Pole.

Then began the famous Boer War, the stages of which everyone followed. And then I remember the day when Father took a large illustrated Bible to the bookbinders. When I was born, Father took a subscription to a weekly magazine called "The Pictorial of the Village Library", and now he had been a subscriber for five years. Each issue contained a section of the Bible, running in order from the very beginning, so that one could collect the sections. They had page numbers and they were lavishly illustrated. The pages were 12 by 12 inches in size. The result was a beautiful hard-cover Bible which I inherited. (But a few years ago I donated it to the "Finnish historical museum" in St. Paul.)

Then religious sects began to gain a lot of ground. One did not go to the state church very often. The only reason for one to go to the church might be to partake in the Holy Communion, because the church did not allow any sect to perform it. And because one still had to pay church tax, religious assembly rooms were built everywhere, and the sects that could not afford one held their meetings in private homes. Of course I was taken along to these meetings, and there I saw plenty of things to wonder about, because there were women crying everywhere in these assembly rooms. I should be crying, I thought, but I didn't feel like crying, not even Uncle Lönroos's departure to America seemed sad enough now to bring tears into my eyes. But then I thought of a way, I pressed my head to the bench, spat a little in my fingers, wiped my eyes with my fingers, then tried to look very sad, and so figured I was looking as I should be.

Christmas came, and several young friends invited me to come and see their Christmas tree. I always came home very sad, but I don't think anyone noticed. I was wondering why I did not have a Christmas tree. Was a Christmas Tree so much against my parents' religion, or did they think I would not understand anything about Christmas trees yet. I kept thinking of ways to get my own Christmas tree. In the kitchen there was a bench with a hole in one end, in which a stand for winding up wool could be set up. A lot of fir branches had been placed in front of the door, and I picked out a single pretty branch, and wrapped paper around its stem so I could make the branch stay upright in the hole in the bench. I admired it even as such, feeling overjoyed that now I too had a Christmas tree. Then I remembered that I had pretty pieces of paper in a box. I had saved the wrapping paper every time I had received a nicely wrapped present from my Uncle, or someone. I used them to decorate my tree as best I could, then I even went and got some cookies from the cupboard and tied them to my tree with pretty bits of string. Now my Christmas tree was finished, and though I had not even thought of candles, I just stood there admiring it as if some beautiful work of art, when Mother entered the kitchen. She looked at me and my tree in turn, began to say something, and said, like a sleep walker, "Anni, you", but her voice was drowned out by sobs. She wiped her eyes with her apron, and went quickly into another room. The Christmas Eve went quickly and we had lots of fun and activities. Finally, exhausted, we would retire between fresh, clean-smelling white sheets in our beds. The organist Himanko was spending his Christmas with us, because two vacation days was not long enough for him to travel home up north. He was also in his room, and all lights had been switched off everywhere in the house, but still some murmuring could be heard, because doors to each room were left either open or ajar. "Hello Urho", I shouted. "Is something the matter, Little Anni", he asked. "Could you get up and play us a Christmas carol, in the dark", I asked. "Why, of course", he answered. "What would you like to hear?" "Could you please play and sing:

No onko tullut kesä	Why, has summer come
nyt talven keskelle.	in the middle of winter
Ja laitetaanko pesä	And shall we make a nest
myös pikku linnuille.	for small birds
Ja kuusi kynttilöitä	And the Christmas tree is blossoming
on käynyt kukkimaan.	with candles
Pimeitä talven teitä	Thus we may brighten
Näin ehkä valaistaan.	the dark winter roads

Of course I had to sing along with the music and soon afterwards I fell asleep, to wake up happy in the morning of the Christmas Day.

In Finland, the snow is wonderful! It is so easy to build snow castles from it. Children from neighboring houses would come to our yard, and we would begin to build. Our efforts produced a spacious, high-walled castle. Even grownups could stand up in it. We built the roof by putting thin wooden slats across from one wall to another and then we covered them with lots of snow. Inside the castle, we crafted a table and a couple of seats. We made holes in the walls to act as windows, and Mother gave us some candles to light up in our castle after dark. Then we went outside the castle to admire how wonderfully beautiful it looked, straight out of a fairytale, in all it's illumination..

Sometimes we would engage in a good and proper snow war, and I remember a poem about it:

Voi kuin nyt on lumi nuoskaa	Oh now the snow is "nuoska"
Nyt joutukaa jo lapset, juoskaa!	Come quickly, children, run!
Kalle, Pekka, Heikki,	Kalle, Pekka, Heikki,
Tulkaa, tulkaa lumisille.	Come, come join a snow war
Minä jo viskaan aika pallon	I going to toss quite a large snow ball
suuren niinkuin miehen kallon	large like a grown man's skull
Riston niskaan.	down Risto's neck.
Huh-huh-huu	Uh oh uh oh
Nyt on lunta täynnä suu.	I got a mouth fulll of snow

(To be continued)

Episode 5, 16 Jul 1954

Älä itke ole vait,	Don't cry, be quiet,
tyydy siihen minkä sait.	settle for what you got.
Juhani ja Kalle käyvät painimaan	Juhani and Kalle begin wrestling,
Jussi jäikin alle,	Jussi ended up in the bottom
nyt lunta päälle vaan.	let's cover him with snow.

24

Jussin vastaostettu uusimekko	Jussi's newly bought coat
on kuin veestä nostettu.	looks as if it were lifted from water
Kädet käyvät kohmeeseen,	Hands begin to freeze
Lähdetään pois huoneeseen.	let's go inside now.
Enää ei saa nakata,	No more snow war,
jo on aika lakata.	now it's time to stop.

The winter, with its activities and games, was nearing its end. One night, I was sitting quietly and wondering to myself, why are double panes put in the windows for the winter, and how come they do not freeze even in the coldest weather? I recalled how Mother prepared to fit in the double panes in the autumn, and that she placed a glass containing some liquid resembling water on the sill between each pair of glass panes. She also sprinkled brick shards on the sill. Then she covered the whole sill with shinning white cotton, and placed some paper flowers over the cotton. Then the double panes were fitted in place, not on the outside like here, but on the inside. Gaps along the frames were sealed with sticky tape. During the winter, the glasses filled up with water, no doubt condensed from vapor, keeping the windows from freezing and fogging up.

In the spring, all sorts of epidemics began to rage, and I could not avoid getting my share of all of them. When I was sick, Father tried to comfort me, saying come spring I would surely get better, and he sang to me about spring:

Nyt on talvi laannu raivoomasta,	Now winter has stopped its raging
Sulain talven lumet vähenee,	The snows of the winter are melting away
Kevään suloa joutuu taivahasta,	Sweet spring descends from heavens
Päivä metsää, vettä suutelee.	Daylight kisses the forests and waters
Koht' on suvi aallot liikkehessä.	Soon summery waves will start rolling

One day, Mother said that I would be going to the countryside for a couple of weeks, where, she reckoned, my health would surely be restored. As soon as Father came home from his errands, I ran to meet him, shouting, all excited: "Mother said I'm going to the country." Father extended his hand to me, and said: "Well, good-bye then, in case there's no time when you are leaving."

I was ever so peeved, thinking Father was just making fun of my trip. But it did come true, and on a beautiful spring day Father took me to the country, to the Kivistö manor. There was so much to see, and the mistress of the Kivistö manor was ever so kind. She had no children of her own, yet she was always willing to answer my questions, however silly many of them must have seemed. All kinds of animals caught my attention there. A beautiful little foal was sprinting around the yard, making me recall and recite a poem I had learned:

Mun varsan on niin sorja	My foal is so graceful,
ja kaunis käydessään,	and so beautiful his gait
Mun varsan on niin norja	My foal is so nimble
ja liukas liikkeiltään.	and so fleet on his feet.
Jos ohe pyrit milloin	Should you try to pass him by,
se eipä laskekkaan.	well, he is not likely to let you.
Korvillaan vilkkaa silloin	He'll flap his ears then,
ja kuopii jaloillaan.	and paw the ground with his hooves.

The most fascinating place in the Kivistö manor was the dairy room. There were milk pots and containers of all sizes, shiny and clean. A long shelf was full of glass pots for viili, curd milk. Even the smell of fresh milk was so pleasant. In the dairy room, Matron put the curds in wooden cheese forms to set, and when the cheeses were done and poured onto plates, the form had made pretty patterns in the cheese. The matron wrapped these cheeses in pieces of white cloth, and they were delivered to the town market.

During my outdoors walks, I also encountered

sheep, and I was just about to scoot off in a hurry, scared that they would charge at me, when Matron saw me running, and she shouted that I did not have to be afraid of them. So I told her about my experiences with that sheep in town. She found my story most amusing, and she said that the next day she was going to shear the sheep, and she was hoping I would help. I promised I would, even though the very idea seemed scary. When I came out the next morning, Matron was already out in the yard, sitting and holding a sheep on her lap, with a large basket for the wool on one side. When I had come near enough, she asked me to sit down next to her and grab hold of the sheep's foot. I actually trembled with fear, but I decided to be brave, and soon I regained my former cheerfulness, and I recited to Matron the following dialog between a sheep and pig:

"Suus kiinni irvihammas"

sialle lihavalle lausui lammas,

Kun yhdessä he vietiin kumpikin.

Niin vastas sika:
"Syyt on huutaa mulla;

mikäpä hätä veikko kulta on sulla.

Sä syliin pääsete,

"Shut your mouth, you fanged beast," to a fat pig said a sheep, as they were rounded up together.

The pig replied: "I have cause to scream, while you, dear friend, have none

You will be held

28

	on lap
villas keritään	you will be sheared
ja sitten vapahaks' sä päästetään.	then they let you free again.
Mutt' huomenna	But come tomorrow,
mä paistiks leikataan."	they'll cut me up into steaks and chops.

What I found especially amazing here in the country was how they got water, as there were no water pipes anywhere. In the yard, they had some contraption with levers drawing water up from a deep well, with a large basin standing next to it. Matron said that was where the animals drank water in the winter, but now they drank from the creek out in their pasture. She promised to draw water into the basin so that I could swim there. I wanted to see the creek, too, and, wandering around the pasture, I finally found it. I spent a lot of time, it was so much fun to kneel by the water and wash dolls' clothes.

I wanted so much to go barefoot, as in town I was never allowed but I banged my toes against rocks so often that my shoes no longer fit, because the good Matron of Kivistö wrapped my toes in thick bandages. And I did not always remember to avoid nettles, either.

This made me remember a poem about nettles:

| Nokkoselle poljetulle | To a trampled nettle |
| ruusu lausui oksaltaan: | a rose said, from |

29

Kov' on onni suotu sulle,

sua aina kartetaan.

Sinuhun ei silmää luoda,

ken sun näkee, väistyy pois.

Hyväilyst' ei sulle suoda,

sillä kättä polttaa vois.

Tuohon vastas nokkonen:

Mutt' sä petät kaunoinen,

Kaikkia sa viittoilet,

sua riemuin poimimahan

Piikkis' piillät, hymyilet,

kyllä kerskaat, ett' on sulla

väri, loisto, jolla kiillät,

mutta julmempi kuin mulla

sull' on miekka, jolla viillät.

its branch:
A hard life were
you granted
you are always
shunned.
Eyes are not cast
upon you,
who sees you,
avoids you
Caresses are not
given to you,
for hands might
get burned.
The nettle
retorted:
But you, oh
pretty one, are
deceitful
You beckon
everyone
to come and
pick you with joy.
You hide your
thorns, you smile,
you brag that
you possess
color, glamor, to
shine with,
but more cruel
than mine
is your slashing
sword.

I went for walks in the beautiful glade, making

many observations. Summer in the country was so wonderful, it was simply marvellous. In the evening, I came to a place which was wide open like a playing ground; flat and green, with a large, sturdily built swing standing at its edge. I thought this must be where the young people gather to have fun. I sat on a tree stump at the clearing's edge, and soon young folk, girls and boys began to arrive. (Bear in mind that in Finland, summer nights are bright.) They did not notice me, and I sat quietly, waiting to see how they were going to pass the evening.

They began to dance and sing:

Hih-hei nyt sinäkin	Hey hey, why don't you
Käyppä kanssani rinkihin.	join us in the ring.
Laulu ihastuttaa	Songs are delightful
nuorten vilkkautta	and cheer up the young
Silmät ilost' loistaa,	Eyes shine with joy
koska toinen toistaan	when one may whirl another
Saapi leikeissä liehuttaa,	round and round in the dance
saapi leikeissä liehuttaa.	round and round in the dance.

They sang several similar pretty little circle dance songs, of which I recall this one, among others:

Kullan sain, kullan sain,	I got a

siit' on hyvä mieli	sweetheart, I got a sweetheart it makes me so happy
Käy, käy kanssani tanssimaan,	Come, come and dance with me
Ei nyt kestä, ei nyt kestä	No longer still, no longer still,
Jalat paikallaan.	feet can no longer stay still.

(To be continued)

Episode 6, 20 Jul 1954

Then some of the youngsters left the round game and went to the swing. They saw me standing at the edge of the clearing and asked me to join them. At first I did not dare, but after a while I mustered my courage and joined them. Soon the wild speed of the swing started to make me dizzy, and suddenly I fell off the swing. I was lucky not to get hurt, but I did get quite a scare. Without looking back I ran to the manor, and, sneaking quietly into my room, went straight to bed. Not even next morning did I say a word of my adventures to anyone, though I was nursing a few sore spots, even bruises, so mostly I was just being quiet in the kitchen and playing with the cat in the kitchen. The mistress stopped to talk to me for a moment, saying I reckon Anni must be a bit homesick, for being so quiet. As she sat down close by with some handicraft, I said, how about I recite you another poem, this time about a cat.

Ikävän nyt kerron teille,

mirri sairastui.
Paha oli ilma eilen,

mirri vilustui.

Nyt on vaivaa ystävällä;

senhän arvaakin.

Pää on kipeänä hällä,

nenä, varpaatkin.

Minä häntä silittelin,

ei se hyrrännyt.

Maidollakin mairittelin,

ei se lerkkinyt.

Äiti makkarankin osti,

mirrilleni vei.

Mirri päätänsä vain nosti,

sanoi, "Kiitos ei."

I have sad news
to tell you
Mirri has taken ill.
The weather was
bad yesterday,
Mirri caught a
cold.
Now the little
friend is suffering,
as one well
might guess.
Its head is
aching,
so is its nose,
even its toes.
I was a-stroking
her,
but she didn't
purr.
I tempted her
with milk,
but she didn't
drink any.
Mother even
brought some
sausages
and took it to my
cat.
Mirri merely lifted
her head,
said, "No, thank
you."

"That was a lovely poem", said the mistress, "goodness but you know a great many poems, and I reckon you are making some yourself". "No, I don't", I said, flustered at the compliment, "I just have a good memory".

Soon afterwards Father came to take me back home to town. Fortunately my toes had healed so that my shoes fit my feet again. Father thanked the mistress of Kivistö for everything, and was happy that I had regained my health. I heard the mistress say that I had been a lot of fun, and that I would be welcome again next summer. During the summer, the religious movements had grown ever stronger. My parents and neighbors went to meetings almost every night. It was difficult to take me along every time, but it was also impossible to leave me home alone, so my parents decided to find a foster sister to keep me company. That is how Maria became the fourth member of our family. Maria was five years older, a very pretty blue-eyed girl. Still Mother didn't quite dare leave us home by ourselves, but she would take us next door. The neighbors had a daughter called Hilda who was soon to be of age. She had already started studying painting at the Ateneum. And she had twin brothers of the same age with me, called Niil and Vilho. Hilda took very motherly care of us younger children while our parents were out. She taught us all kinds of games, and she told us stories, and described funny incidents from her school. Hilda had an excellent memory for detail. She would tell us about the things she had seen in town, then draw us a picture of the whole incident so that we would see it as if through her eyes. When she went to the theater, she remembered the recital and drew us pictures of it. She drew for us such a

34

good likeness of the Finnish theater's star actress Aino Acté that we recognized her picture in the newspapers. It was no wonder Hilda had decided to become a painter. We talked a great deal about the school year starting at autumn, for I was finally due to start school, and together we sang:

Eipä kesä aina kestä vaan	Summer does not last for ever
syksyn tuuli nyt jo puit' puistaa	now the autumn wind is shaking the trees.
Koulutietä taaskin astutaan,	We shall start school again,
vaikeatkin läksyt täytyy muistaa.	we must remember even the hardest subjects.
Hyvästi siis kaikki metsät,	So, good-bye, all woods,
marjamaat,	all fields where berries grow.
Lukukirjan kannet avata nyt saa.	Now we may open our ABC books.
Eipä kesä aina kestä vaan,	Summer does not last for ever
syksyn tuuli nyt jo puita puistaa.	now the autum wind is shaking the trees.

PART II: SCHOOL YEARS, EPISODES 6-11

I shall start this part of my story with a song:

Mä kouluun aamulla läksin varhain	Early in the morning I left for school
hojenkauttajapuutarhain.	through fields and gardens
Ja purot, pensakat, puut, ja aita	Brooks, bushes, trees and fences
Ne kaik' oli tuttuja arvokkaita.	were all familiar and dear.
Mä käyskelin ja laulelin	I was walking and singing to myself,
Ja lyhyt vain oli matkakin.	and the distance was short.
Taas saman tien kävin iltamalla	I took the same route at night
Epäillen, vaiti ja hapumalla.	hesitant, quiet and fumbling around.
Yö peittää mun mä sokeun, ja kodin porttihin kompastun.	Night drowns me it blinds me and I stumble over our garden gates.

Here, at least in the countryside, all children in a village go to the same school, but back there in Finland in the big towns children are sent to different schools. My foster sister Maria had to go to a school that was quite far away from our home, while my

38

school was only two streets down. Our neighbor's twin boys went to yet another school, so every night we had a lot to talk about our schools. However we all had one thing in common. The very first thing we were taught was Our Land:

Oi maamme, Suomi, synnyinmaa	Oh, our land, Finland, country of birth
soi sana kultainen.	so rings the golden word.
Ei laaksoa, ei kukkulaa, ei vettä, rantaa rakkaampaa	No valley, no hill, no water, no shore is dearer
kuin kotimaa tää pohjoinen	than this northern home country,
maa kallis isien.	beloved land of our fathers.

We were forty girls and boys in my classroom. The same building housed two other classes, with the same number of students, so altogether we were a hundred and twenty first-graders to receive teaching in Finnish. On the other side of the school yard there were as many classrooms and as many children who would be taught in Swedish.

When they let us all out at recess, it certainly made quite a racket with all two hundred and forty pupils in the yard at the same time. Both languages were used in the games. The curious thing, though, was that the Swedish language won. All children sang all playground songs in Swedish. I, too, learned them all, and I still remember one of them quite well, though

I'm not at all sure about the spelling:

Kom kom fager ugersven	Come, come handsome young men
Kom föra oss båda i dansen	lead us both to dance
Den ena giver jag en krog	One fellow, I shall turn down
Den andra tar jag i min borg	The other, I shall take to my castle
Där är glädje och ingen sorg	There will be joy and no sorrow
Där skall bröllopet hällas	There we shall have a wedding

I paid a lot less attention to home matters now, because school took plenty of time, and even at home I would be thinking only of school. However I did notice that Mother was not as happy as before, though Maria's presence still gave her a lot of joy, Maria being so clever and beautiful that she could have captured even the coldest heart. Had I realized, I would have had plenty of cause to envy the beautiful Maria, who nowadays got Mother's attention almost exclusively, nothing was too good for Maria, and soon Maria realized her power over Mother. Often, when Maria got into trouble, she would quickly say it was Anni's fault, and I, not defending myself, received all scoldings, sometimes even a spanking, while completely innocent.

Mother cried often, and not even the carefree chatter of the merry Maria helped Mother to forget her worries. Even Father had grown more serious, and

40

it was much less often now that he would recite or sing something for me. Gradual changes were taking place, and I could not understand why.

(To be continued)

Episode 7, 23 Jul 1954

Maria had been very bad; I found out, though it seemed they tried to keep it a secret. She had gone in the store and taken money from the cash register, without permission, and she had been given a right proper spanking.

I was no longer taking piano lessons, as I was much more interested in learning how to knit and crochet. I learned very easily, and I became so keen on knitting that even when other children came over to play, I would just sit there, knitting. One day Maria came to ask me to join the play, then the visiting children rushed in, and someone came too close and bumped into me accidentally, of course, and one of the knitting sticks went up my nose. Maria tried to pull it out but failed. The stick was firmly stuck. She started screaming for help. I do not know what happened next. I had passed out and woke up on my bed; the visiting children had gone. That put an end to my knitting fancy for a long time.

However after a while I wanted to try crocheting, but that met with similar misfortune. By the time that happened, I had become quite good at crocheting and thus was too keen to want to stop even when other children came near me to play. The crochet hook got stuck under the nail of my thumb, and nobody, including me, thought to turn the hook so that it would have been easy to pull out. Then someone picked me up and carried me half a block down to the smith's where they were able to detach the hook.

The first school year went quickly, and I remember little about it besides that whispering in class was strictly forbidden. One day one of the children sitting behind me was whispering, and the teacher assumed it was me. Without asking a single question, the teacher walked up to me and slapped me across the cheek so hard I shall never forget it. And it was unthinkable to be allowed to say a word in my own defense. Afterwards I was thinking to myself that the poor teachers probably would not have managed at all without strict discipline, seeing as each of them had forty pupils to teach. And so I forgave the teacher for that injustice, though I can never forget it, for as long as I shall live.

One day the teacher declared that on a certain night just before Christmas, ten pupils with the best grades would be allowed to come to the school house and help decorate the Christmas tree, and, oh, the joy when I turned out to be one of them. Time went so slowly, waiting for that special night, but finally it arrived, and it was so much fun to be allowed to put up decorations in the big tree according to the teacher's instructions. The teacher even gave us some candy, which, together with the bustling around the beautiful Christmas tree created such a light and festive mood that it reminded me of a part of poem that Father had once recited:

Ja iso-äiti aukaisi salin oven   And

sepposeljälleen,
ja valo tuli kuusen kynttilöistä,

että oikein silmiä huikiasi.

grandmother
opened the hall
door
wide open,
and the candles
on the tree
shone so bright
that it rightly
blinded the eyes.

One day I went to show Father a tooth that was being very troublesome, it just was not coming loose. Father said that there was only one thing to do, to go to the dentist. "All alone", I asked. — "Oh, for sure", he replied, "you are a big girl now, going on six, and you must learn to trust yourself. I shall come with you part of the way, but you must go in by yourself." He gave me a one-mark coin which I carefully wrapped in the corner of my handkerchief. Then we walked up to the door where a sign read: "Äyräpää Hammaslääkäri". My knees were trembling when I opened the door and went in. I was so nervous that I cannot remember how the tooth was pulled out, but I do remember how I took the one-mark coin from inside the handkerchief, and the dentist wrapped the tooth in tissue paper, then tied it inside the handkerchief and gave it to me. I ran all the way home thinking that father was right: one can manage if only one trusts oneself.

One day Maria was not around when Mother needed her help, she must have gone next door. So Mother asked me to run the errand instead, seeing as I had been to the store several times before. I always went to Sandra and Fanni's store, where the good ladies carefully read my shopping list and wrapped everything up properly. Then they would make a small paper cone and put in some candy, giving it to me as a "bonus".

As Mother was giving me an errand to run, I asked for the shopping list. She said, "You won't need a list, just bring a kilo of wheat semolina." I rushed off, repeating to myself, wheat semolina, wheat semolina. A friend from school saw me and asked me where I was going in such a hurry. I told her I was doing some shopping for Mother and ran on. The moment I got in the store I told the "puukhollari", that's the assistant, "a kilo of rice semolina, please". I rushed back home and gave the bag to Mother. She opened it, gave me an angry stare, saying, "I asked you to bring wheat semolina". Then she asked what else I got up to while running the errand. "Well, I saw Alli and stopped for a second to talk to her before I went to the store, and that is why I could not remember exactly what kind of semolina it was supposed to be", I replied.

The first school year went quickly. So did the short summer holidays in the Koivistö manor. During the second school year something seemed to be wrong at home. I heard talk about large sums of money, "guarantees". What on earth were they? — The word "bankruptcy" appeared in my parents' discussions, very ominous. I was very frightened when I saw Mother gathering our clothes, her eyes in tears. Finally I mustered enough courage to ask what was going on. At first Mother was reluctant to tell, saying it was no use as I would not begin to understand, but then she began to speak: "Now we must move to a small town north of here and live there, because Father has lost everything we had. We may take only some clothes and personal items with us."

In complete good faith, Father, with a colleague of his, had guaranteed a loan for another businessman, but the colleague slipped quietly to America, leaving Father to pay back the full amount alone, and when the loan was due, we had no choice but to sell everything and pay. So we moved to a small town, and a small apartment, trying to start over, but Mother began to wither before our very eyes. She had a dry cough.

Father took a job as a traveling salesman, and was home very seldom. Maria was growing ever more beautiful, and very "adult", despite her age. People no longer called her Maria, but Miss Södergren. She was very good at school, and soon she had completed her studies as far as Father could afford to finance them. Then all she had to do was to help Mother at home. My school here in a small town was very different. At school my favorite subject was handicrafts, that's where I got my best grades. I also stood out in gymnastics, because I was very brisk and agile.

My schooling continued, and certain subjects became my great favorites. I especially liked arts, handicrafts and gymnastics. I got so excited about gymnastics that I decided to become the best gymnast at school, a goal which I succeeded in achieving.

(To be continued)

Episode 8, 27 Jul 1954

Then a special sewing circle was set up at school, meeting once a week, in the evening. We made socks and sweaters for sailors. Completed items were wrapped in parcels, and the maker's name and address was included, so that we maybe might find out where our handicrafts ended up, but no recipient's name, because the seaman's association took the parcels and distributed them according to their own lists. Some time after the parcels had been mailed, letters started to arrive to the addresses in the parcels. The girls brought the letters to the sewing circle meetings and the teacher read them out loud. There were some really nice letters from faraway countries where young Finnish seamen were feeling homesick, waiting to be homeward bound, and they described how nice it was to receive a parcel. Soon the letters started declaring burning love — well, how could the poor boys have realized that the parcels came from young schoolgirls. Some letters made the teacher blush, and soon she shut down the sewing circle altogether and strictly forbade us to reply to a single letter.

That year Finland got a new Governor-General, and thus began for us the famous "Bobrikoff era". Several prominent politicians were exiled to Siberia to face an unknown future, without any excuse or explanation. Very few relatives ever heard a word from the exiled. Fear took hold of people. Mother forbade us to discuss anything related to the government, and we were only supposed to whisper.

But Finland stood proud:

Kuin Pohjan kuusi talvella

Se vihannoi,

Like a Northern fir in the winter
it is ever green

vaikk' myrsky soi	even in a raging storm
Ja pelton se pystys on,	it stands proud, fearless,
ei säiky valtaa kohtalon.	it fears not the powers of fate.

One night, we were again waiting for Father to come home, stifled with fear. The doorbell rang and Mother went to answer the door. We were certain it was Father, but instead it was a big man in impressive official dress, introducing himself as the "viskaali" in charge, and he wanted to know where Father was. Mother was unable to tell where Father was at that time, because he traveled around a lot; the official left, and we got off with a mere fright.

At school, more than ever, we were taught patriotism and bravery, they were the subjects of all poems and songs. More than ever, Finland was under the oppression of a great power, under the rule of a true Finland-eater, Bobrikoff. There was not a single child old enough to speak who would not utter that name without disdain.

But regardless of oppression, Finnish culture flourished. In the poet's fitting words:

Kesken talven pakkasta	In the middle of the coldest winter
voipi kansa kukkia.	a nation can blossom.
Kesken hankien ja jään	Amidst snow drifts and ice
henki tekee tähkäpään.	spirit comes to

fruition.

The fervor of patriotism continued in my school. We learned each and every one of "Second lieutenant Stål's Songs" by heart, and the poem titled "Number Fifteen, Stolt" which tells about a brave Finnish youngster, became our great favorite. Everyone tried to recite it with just the right emphasis. And we would sing "The Soldier boy" so that the walls of the school house would shake. But there were other songs, too, harder to learn, and the music teacher had to keep repeating them over and over, which made the music teacher so mad as to yell, "You are a bunch of Hottentots and gypsy children."

Bobrikoff kept issuing new orders. The Russian language replaced Swedish as the second language in most offices. Signs with Finnish and Swedish street names were taken down from street corners and replaced with Russian and Finnish signs. We thought the Russian signs looked funny. It was proposed that schools teach Russian, German or Swedish, two out of those three languages. Of course we rejected Russian, since it was not compulsory.

After the terrible financial "crash", Father was starting to get back on his "feet" again. He opened stores in a couple of small towns and was able to spend more time at home. Mother was giving Maria whatever she wanted to have. Father noticed it and told Mother not to, but Mother kept on fulfilling Maria's every wish. She even gave Maria a key, so Maria could get in at whatever time of the night she happened to come home. Then Maria wanted to go the confirmation school though she was not yet old enough. Mother went to discuss the matter with the vicar; she told him that Maria was going abroad and that Mother wanted Maria to finish the confirmation school first. And so Maria got to go to the confirmation school a year early, and Mother's breast was fairly heaving with joy and happiness as she watched her picture-perfect Maria partake of the Holy Communion, in front of the altar. Probably upon Mother's request, Father bought a beautiful silver watch and presented it to Maria as a confirmation school present.

Maria wanted to get out of the house and earn some money. Father agreed, and so Maria started working in a factory. She even bought some presents on the wages she had earned, and this time we put up a big Christmas tree a couple of days before Christmas. We had had a proper Christmas tree ever since that Christmas when I built myself a tree out of a single fir branch. A month before Christmas Father had told Mother that he wanted to organize a feast for all his employees and their families.

Maria came home several days earlier, to help Mother with the preparations. A load of necessary tableware was collected from the storekeeper. A large hall on the other side of the yard was decorated very festively. Long tables and benches were set in the middle, complete with shining white table clothes.

When all the delicious food was ready and the hall was full of guests, the party began with a speech given by the employees' spokesman, but unfortunately I did not understand a single word. Then, on behalf of all employees, he presented Father with a large picture. Everyone cheered, and Father responded with a couple of words. Children were brought to our apartment, and we played around the

Christmas tree. Mother had provided small Christmas presents, and we sang Christmas carols together.

But then unhappy times returned. Often, when I came home from school, the doctor was there. Still, the spring seemed a more hopeful time. Lighter evenings lured young people outdoors. Maria would often sit on the steps in front of the house, with girlfriends, chatting and singing patriotic songs.

Love songs, too, such as this one:

Hiljaa juur' kuin lammin laine	Gently, like a wave in the pond
syttyi lempeni ainainen.	arose my everlasting love
Syntyy lämmöstä kevätpäivä	From warmth, spring day is born
kera kaunisten kukkasten.	with its beautiful flowers.

When Maria sang another song in her beautiful voice, even Father stopped to listen, his expression serious. Father never got tired of this particular song. Maria sang:

Kas Suomenlahdella hyrskyt	The surging waves of the Gulf of Finland
ja laajat Laatokan veet,	and the wide waters of the Lake Ladoga
ja vuolaan Tornion tyrskyt	and the swelling flow of the River

	Tornio
ja maansilän harjanteet	the ridges of Maanselkä
Ne halkoo Suomea suurta	They split up the great Finland
ja pilkkoo kansaa sen.	and divide her people
Ne katkovat sammon juurta,	They break up the roots of the sampo
ei juurru se uudelleen.	and it cannot put down roots again.

And the last verses of that song:

Vaan syntyä voisi silta	If only a bridge could be built
mi kansani yhteen tois.	that would reunite my people.

It actually brought tears into Father's eyes, because the future of the Finnish people seemed utterly hopeless under the thumb of the "Ryssä" Bobrikoff.

Before Maria and her friends said good-night to each other, they sang one last song:

On tyyni nyt yön hellä henki,	The night's gentle breeze calms down
se povellensa painoi maan.	holding all land to its breast

Nyt vait' on lehdon lintunenkin

ja oksalle käy nukkumaan.

Even the birds in
the glades grow
quiet
and settle on the
branches to
sleep.

(To be continued)

Episode 9, 30 Jul 1954

Maria went back to the factory, but was seldom at home at night. One night when Father was at home, Maria did not return until well past midnight. She opened the door quietly with her own key. Father woke up, saw the time and well, that ended all peace and quiet for that night. Father was so angry that he told Maria to move out first thing in the morning. It was a harsh blow to Mother, but she did not dare say a word. Father's word was the law in our house.

Maria did come and visit Mother often, and one day she told Mother that a couple of young girls had decided to go to Stockholm, where there were plenty of good jobs available, and that she would like to go, too. Mother agreed soon, though unhappy, and furnished Maria with everything she would need. Soon the departure day dawned, and mothers went to the station to see their daughters off. When Mother came home, she said, her eyes in tears, "Maria was the prettiest girl of all those who were leaving, and she received more flowers than anyone else from those who came to say good-bye." And so it was that joy died in Mother's eyes, voice, and of course her heart, too. She started coughing more and more. All doctors were tried, and so were all possible and impossible remedies and cures, even magic.

One night I was just about to finish my homework, when Mother came and stood next to my chair; I looked up into her sad eyes, and she said, "Would you like to do me a small favor?" "Why of course," I answered.

She gave me a small piece of paper on which there were three small pieces of bread, and said: "They have a spell in them". Two streets down there was a big public water pump where people got their drinking water, because it was better for that purpose than the water in the municipal water system. Now Mother said, "Make sure that nobody sees you or follows you (and it was a right dark autumn night), go to the water pump and toss the bread crumbs over the pump, one at a time, then come back quickly, and be very sure not to look back even once."

I did exactly as Mother told me to, and she was waiting for me at the door, almost feverish. She explained that it was a cure, so if her cough was caused by the water, it would end now. "Let's believe it is so", I said simply.

Soon I forgot the whole affair. Mother kept on coughing, and growing worse, but I had so much to do that I was not paying much attention. I had to get up at six o'clock every morning, and go to the market place to buy milk, meat, and whatever food we needed for the day. Back at home, I had to eat quickly, change into my school clothes, and practically run to the school several blocks away, where I had to be at eight o'clock, even on Saturdays.

Finally Mother had to stay in bed all day, and

we had to get a housekeeper so I did not have to do so many chores, and this helped me make much better progress at school. Mother wanted to get up and come to the Christmas party at school, where awards were given to the best pupils. When they announced my name, I walked as if in a dream, but with my eyes all shining, up to the front where the head of all schools gave me my award: a Bible. I said thank you, curtsied, and took the Bible to my Mother, bursting into tears, to the sound of enormous applause. It was probably the first time, and the last, when Mother was proud of me, and I had to wonder whether, even then, she was thinking about Maria, whom she had regarded better than anyone else, always, and at everything.

We did not know then that we were spending our last Christmas with Mother. It was such a quiet Christmas, because Mother was bedridden for the most of the day, though occasionally she seemed a bit better, especially on the days when there was a letter from Maria.

I sat thinking about past Christmases, remembering especially clearly the Christmas five years ago. Around then I had become pretty good at knitting socks, so I knitted a pair of socks for Father, wrapped them up, and wrote my name on the parcel. Then I got the key to my Father's desk, put my present in the drawer, locked the drawer and put the key back in its place.

But then curiosity won. Because I was home alone, I decided to take a peek, thinking I was not going to take anything, or touch anything, just look. I figured that since I had opened one drawer, I had to see what was kept in the large cabinets below. I got

54

the key out again and opened the cabinets. The lock, or both locks, unlocked easily, quietly, and holding my breath I peeked inside both cabinets. There were stacks of men's clothes, underwear, socks, scarves, and a large brown, important looking official envelope. I held it in my hands for a moment, wondering whether I would dare take a look at its contents. I opened it, and there were carefully folded papers, a passport to America and a photograph of my Father. Hastily, I replaced everything and put back the key, but for several days I felt as if I were ill, thinking I had been prying into secrets I was not supposed to know about.

This had taken place five years ago, when Mother was still fairly healthy, but now she was in bed, quiet and ill. Now that I was thinking about that incident, I was amazed that I had been so stupid in the first place as to put my present to Father in a locked-up drawer, for that was certainly not what Santa Claus did with presents, and I actually blushed with shame thinking how stupid I had been. Every Christmas I was afraid that Father would say something, especially when Christmas presents came up in discussion. My conscience was also scolding me for looking at the contents of the locked cabinets, for seeing things I was not supposed to see.

On one of our frequent walks, Father told me the secret of the writing desk. He said"As you know," (I blushed but did not respond), "for a few years, I have had all my clothing and passport for America packed up and ready to go, or from when life seemed so hopeless after losing everything, and it was hard to start over. So I was planning to disappear quietly, but then your mother grew more ill, and besides I could not leave you." He was quiet for a moment. Then he said as if to himself:"And the passports have expired now."

Father told me that because life had seemed totally hopeless five years ago, he had decided to end it all and go to America, that everything had already been in order, even passports, then in the end he could not leave Mother and me after all, but started over, and succeeded. Now, as an eleven-year-old, I understood it all much better. Thank God, Father never said a word about "socks", perhaps he thought that he had left the drawer open and that I had put them there by accident. And so he never got to learn what I had done, first out of stupidity, then in curiosity.

We had a visitor. She had known my parents for a long time and knew the life and times of our family members well. First she told that she had received a letter from America, from my Uncle Anton Lönroos. Then she said that she had been a close friend to my Aunt Linda ever since childhood, they had gone to school together, and grown up together. I was listening very carefully to her story, wondering whether she would say anything more about the reasons that had made Uncle Lönroos to leave for America, because I remembered Uncle's departure and even a fragment of the discussion between Uncle and Aunt that I had overheard during my visit. Of course our visitor did not realize, while chattering, that "small pots had ears", too.

(To be continued)

Episode 10, 3 Aug 1954

56

The visitor told us how beautiful the pale-skinned, red-haired Aunt Linda had been; and how the two of them secretly admired the handsome, only son of the factory owner. He went to school in the city, and there was talk that he would later go abroad for further studies. But this young man did not think himself above others, so when he was back home from school, he would go to the dance just like the other young people in the village, and there he was always keen on Aunt Linda's company. I knew that my Grandfather was poor and unable to afford much in the way of schooling for his children. Aunt Linda was reluctant to go out with such a rich man, what would everyone say, seeing as she was but the daughter of a poor factory worker. Master Aleksi suggested that Linda and he keep their friendship a secret, but Linda disagreed, even though by then she was so deeply in love with Aleksi that she couldn't sleep at night, and so she suggested that Aleksi come and meet her parents, or else she, Linda, would no longer go out with him. Aleksi agreed, and on one Sunday night he went to visit Linda's parents. When Linda's old father saw Master Aleksi walking towards their house, he got terribly frightened, thinking, surely it was because now the young master must be the new director of the factory, and he was coming to fire him, perhaps even canceling the pension he had been promised, or at least cutting some of it. When Aleksi stepped in and greeted the old man, he thought it best to bring the subject up himself, and perhaps soften the blow that way.

First, however, he asked Linda to go and make some coffee and then he politely asked Master Aleksi to take a seat. Linda's father began, "Well, unhh .... about that pension, well, seeing as I am getting older, so, if you mean you do not need me any longer, then and, well, about the pension." Master Aleksi interrupted him and said, "Even if you stopped working this very moment, your pension payments will start and you will be paid your pension for the rest of your life, but now I have come to talk to you about a matter of much higher importance." Now the old man was looking at Aleksi in absolute fear, but Aleksi continued, "You may have heard that I have been going out with your daughter Linda, and you may have been wondering how it might end. I understand it completely, as Linda is very dear to you and the last of your daughters still living at home, but you need not worry, as although I am but a young man, I am an honorable man. My father wants me to study for many more years, and then go abroad for further engineering studies. I am not going to leave your daughter in this town when I go, as I want to marry her after completing my studies, and Linda has promised to wait for me. But now it is so that Linda and I love each other and Linda has promised to wait for me, but my Father does not approve; you see, he is so conservative that he would prefer to have a "Gentry Damsel" as his daughter-in-law. He does not know Linda and he won't even hear of me bringing Linda to meet him. I must return to school, but I do not wish to leave Linda here, and she has agreed to move to Helsinki and go to a boarding school. I shall pay all expenses, if only you were to give Linda your permission to go. Think about it like this: Linda will receive higher education, and when, upon my graduation, we shall marry, my Father cannot have any more objections." The old man could only nod his head in agreement. "Well that is settled, then", Master Aleksi said, "and now let's shake hands on it". Just then Linda arrived from the kitchen with the coffee tray and instantly she saw in Aleksi's face that the desired outcome had been reached. Soon afterward Aleksi went abroad to study, and Linda organized her clothes to go to school to become "civilized", as she would like to joke.

Our visitor told us all this. We already knew the rest that Aunt Linda had instead gone and married Antoni Lönroos in Helsinki. Master Aleksi had married, too and had children. And then his wife had died a couple of years ago. Now Aleksi owned the entire factory, after his father's death.

One day he traveled to the city on business, and entirely by accident he met Anton Lönroos at a party where they were introduced to each other. Their discussion took such a turn that Aleksi realized that Lönroos was the husband of his former fiancée, and so Aleksi began to "claim back his own", as he put it, even if it were to be against payment. Uncle Lönroos had agreed to accept payment. And that was the period of time I had overheard Aunt Linda refer to with "Aleksi has already put the money in the bank, and you you can travel a month from now." So why had he not traveled that soon? His departure had been delayed by some formalities and the legalization of his divorce. And of course, later, Father and I were at the harbor, seeing Uncle Lönroos off on his trip to America, and soon afterwards Aunt Linda married Aleksi and they bought a large manor as their home. Now Uncle Lönroos had been living on the other side of the ocean for several years, and Aunt

Linda had become Mrs. Aleksi Arnio soon after Uncle's departure, but it was only now that I found out about all these details, from our guest.

Winter was over, and spring was coming so early that one felt like singing with joy:

Touon aika lähenee,
Planting time draws nearer

kylmät hallat vähenee
cold frost strikes less often

Päivä kirkkahasti
The sun shines bright

paistaa ihanasti
korkealta taivahalta,
siintävältä loistavalta.
and wonderful high in the sky, shimmering and beautiful.

Virta vilpas vieriää,
Fresh streams start to flow

järven laine kieriää,
the waves of the lakes start to roll and so on.

I arose from my reverie when Mother spoke up. She said: "Now, Anni, you better write to Maria and ask her to come home." There and then I woke up to the reality, rather than imagination. It was a sad fact that Mother would not be with us for much longer.

I wrote the letter and mailed it at once, and as soon as Maria received Mother's request, she must have guessed that Mother's condition had become hopeless, because within a couple of days Maria came home. In a short time, she had become a real city dweller. Even her voice sounded different, and somehow it no longer seemed proper to address her simply with the familiar "you". Mother must have been happy to have her Maria back, and Maria duly gave Mother all her attention. Nobody really noticed me. I went to school by day and was busy with my homework by night. A couple of weeks passed like this. Often, when I came home from school, I saw the doctor's overcoat in the vestibule. I would creep quietly to my room, so as not to cause any disturbance.

One day, as soon as I got in, I realized that something had happened. Mother had passed away, death had come for her.

Oi tuoni	Oh death
miks' niin julma saatoit olla?	how could you be so cruel
Ett' äitini sa multa riistit pois	that you took my mother away from me
Et sääliä sa mua kohtaan tunne	You feel no pity for me
mun sydämeni alati vaikeroi.	my heart laments for ever.

From that moment on, spring went so slowly, though not much was left of the spring term. I had to force myself to gather my thoughts, as this was my last year in this school, and I wanted to graduate with good grades. Maria returned to Sweden, and Father and I were left alone, except for the housekeeper. I would often hum to myself:

Mun tieni usein	Often, my path
kummun luokse kulkee	goes to the

	grave
Ja siellä aina olla tahtoisin.	and there I would stay forever.
Sen kylmä helma	In its cold embrace
sylihinsä sulkee	it encloses
Mi maailmas' oli	what, in this world,
mulle rakkahin.	I loved the most.
Jos kanssaan siellä	If only with her
uinuella voisin	I could slumber there, too,
Ois' hauska siellä kahden uinua.	we would happily sleep, together.
Sen kylmä helma	Its cold embrace
kyllä meidät suojaa	would shelter us,
Ei lumi sinne pääse tuiskumaan.	in there, snow will never fall.

(To be continued)

Episode 11, 6 Aug 1954

The school graduation became quite an occasion. As the best student, I was awarded the famous Finnish epics "Kalevala" and "Kanteletar", which would have made many a student so very proud, but it did not move me all that much. I no longer had a mother to congratulate me, and Father found no time at all to come to the graduation. In fact, he did not come home until the next day, and even then he was so busy that he never asked how the graduation went. He just said: "Now you must get ready. You will go and stay with Grandfather in that small industrial village". He said he would organize everything for the auction, and, as an aside of sorts, he mentioned that he had renewed the passports, and that now I should enjoy the summer holidays, and continue my studies in the autumn.

He said he had met with his sister, Mrs. Arino. She had asked to have me as her foster daughter, saying it in fact was her duty, as my godmother. This proposal made my father angry. And he said that Aunt Linda better see to her own children, and only then, ask to have other people's children in care. Aunt Linda did not have any children of her own, but she had become the stepmother to the children of Mr. Arnio. There had been no disharmony, but the children had left home and settled here and there. However, one of the boys had returned upon his father's request and promised to spend the summer at the manor of his father and Aunt Linda.

When I arrived, my Grandfather welcomed me so warmly that even my grief felt lighter. Instantly the whole village knew that I was there for the summer, and soon all the villagers greeted me as if they had always known me, the boys would tip their caps, the girls would curtsy neatly, and when my Father arrived a week later to say good-bye to Grandfather and other relatives, I felt pretty much "at home". That same week, Father left for America, and I began to feel that I was

Vain yksin täällä   All alone here
kuin lintu oksalla.   like a bird on a
                                     branch

63

Mä olen niinkuin lintunen

joka metsässä visertää.

Ei ole mulla turvaa,

eik' yhtään ystävää.

And I would sing:
I am like a little
bird
singing in the
woods
I have neither
security
nor a single
friend.

PART III: YOUTH IN FINLAND, EPISODES 11-17

Kun nuoruuden aika on ruusuinen	In the rosy times of youth
ja riemuinen on joka puoli;	when joy surrounds you,
Ota tiestäsi vaari,	Pay heed to your path
ja suunnasta sen	and its direction.
Älä kaikista ruusuista huoli	Do not accept every rose
Ota tiestäsi vaari,	Pay heed to your path
kun muuten se vie	or else it might lead
syvyyksiin, joissa voi kuolla.	to depths where you will die.
Ah, vaaroja täynnä	Oh, fraught with danger
on maailman tie	is the road through the world
Ja kuiluja sen joka puolla.	it is surrounded by gorges.

Grandfather noticed my melancholy, understanding well what it felt like to lose within a few months one's mother, father and home, and he tried hard to cheer me up. He took me to the paper mill, and indeed there was a lot to see. The machines ran on hydroelectric power, generated from the rapids by great turbines. Paper was not made from wood pulp, as it is here, but from rags. On the grounds of the factory there were long rows of wooden buildings. One of the buildings was a long wooden shed where loads of rags were carted. Almost all the older women in the village worked there sorting the rags and cutting off buttons and other hard objects. In those days, it was the best and best-known paper mill in Finland: it manufactured the best paper for government use, and for export. They manufactured fine writing paper, water-stamped sheets and various types of colored paper as well as heavy stock.

Upstream of the dam, water was high and often boys and older men could be seen there, fishing. Middle-aged villagers, women and men alike, worked in the mill by day, so the village seemed very quiet, but by night there was a lot of bustling. On Sundays, there was usually something on at the assembly hall, and then that large hall was full of people. Once I attended a wedding there, and I would not have believed that here, in the countryside, so many lively young people might gather in once place at the same time. It reminded me of a poet's words:

Siis seiso suorana suomalainen	Finns, stand proud,
Sä ole vapaa, jalo Suomen mies.	Finnish man, be free and noble
Sä lemmi, lohduttele Suomen nainen,	Finnish woman, give love and comfort
ja liehdo lämpimäksi kotilies.	and make warm the hearth and home.

That night, when I came home to Grandfather's, he described another wedding, one that he had attended as a young man. The wedding had been a lavish occasion. The groom was very rich, so of course the wedding had to reflect it. The bride was from a poor home, but the groom had bought her a most beautiful wedding gown. The assembly hall was full of guests, but almost every local came to "crash" the party. People were hollering for the bride to come out to the veranda and show herself to the villagers, and so the bride had come out in all her glory, saying, "This is how I look in the front", then she whirled around, adding, "And this is how I look in the back, now hurry up and take a quick look, the gentlefolks are waiting inside."

Here, in my Father's home village, young people had a summer meeting place in the pretty woods on the outskirts of the village. A large platform had been built in the middle, with benches around it. At night, the young villagers would gather there to have fun, play music and sing. Going there, still far away I could already hear the singing:

Laula, kun sull' iloineen	Sing, while with all its joys
nuoruus aukeaapi,	youth embraces you
Sydämestä sydämeen	From one heart to another
Laulun voima saapi.	reaches the power of song
Laulelosi nuoruuden	The songs of your youth,
Kerran syksyn joutuen	as autumn once arrives,
Taasen soivat sulle.	will be played again for you

Isn't it quite something, how the songs spring to mind? For example:

Kuule kuinka soitto kaikuu	Listen to that music
Väinön kanteleesta raikuu,	ringing out from the kantele of Väinö,
Suomen laulua.	the song of Finland.

Often, great sadness would overwhelm me at Grandfather's, though he and everyone else were so good to me, but still the summer seemed to go so slowly that I thought of going to Aunt Linda's, because she had written to me, saying that I would have a good time in their manor home. Her present husband Aleksi loved nature and flowers, thus Aunt Linda thought that Master Aleksi and I would have a lot in common. Aunt Linda remembered my large collection of dried and pressed flowers and plants, reckoning I might "perhaps find some new plants" there.

So I said good-bye and thanked my Grandfather and everyone else for their kindness, and took the train to the town. Aunt Linda welcomed me so warmly that even my melancholy faded away. Here, Aunt Linda found herself in circumstances that were entirely different to those of the high society in the city. Now she was the mistress of a large manor, giving orders to the servant staff with great confidence. It seemed that she was born for this very position, because she handled the servants in such a way that everyone would just smile and say, "Yes, madam", and everything was done ever so smoothly. But she had not forgotten her city friends, as she would often have guests, filling up the spacious rooms most weekends. The manor had very large grounds, mostly pine woods, with pretty paths criss-crossing here and there. There were several small cabins in the woods, far enough from one another for each to have privacy amidst the trees, so that all summer guests could enjoy themselves without any disturbance from their neighbors. Walking around the woods, making my observations, I kept thinking to myself that had those cabins not been built so grandly, they easily could have been from that song, seeing how they were standing in the pine woods.

(To be continued)

Episode 12, 10 Aug 1954

Honkain keskellä	Amidst pines
mökkini seisoo	my cabin stands
Suomeni soreassa salossa.	in a beautiful Finnish forest.
Honkain välistä	Between the pines,
siintävä selkä	a shimmering expanse of water
vilkkuvi koittehen valossa.	glitters in the morning sun

There were in fact two lakes. One of them was really just a small pond that Master Aleksi had seeded with fish, with which he was conducting all sorts of experiments I could not begin to understand. And I was thinking to myself, not daring to ask, yet realizing without asking, that here in the countryside he was happier than back in town, running the paper mill.

The other lake was large and on its shores there were several rowing boats for the summer guests to use. Once a relative, a young girl, arrived for a weekend visit, and it seemed that on her very first night her eyes captured the "vouti", or foreman of the manor. They wanted to go down to the lake, but then Elina, the girl, said that they wanted me and Master Toimi, Aleksi's son with them in the boat. Master Aleksi's son was just one year older than I, always up to some sort of mischief, and he was ready to go to the lake at once.

As soon as Toimi told me to go sit in the front while he went to sit in the back, and the young couple in the middle, I guessed he had something mischievous in mind. The boat glided gently and smoothly on the lake's calm surface, and the youngsters started to sing:

Sun olen vuorten laaksoin erotessa,	I am yours as the mountains rise from the valleys
Vaikk' meren aallot	Even if the waves of the sea
kuinka pauhoaa	crash hard and loud
Hiekkaan peittyy	Covered with sand
liljat erämaassa	become the lilies

	in the desert
Sun olen vaan.	Still I am only
	yours

Then they sang:

Tuudittele tuuli	Wind, rock gently
mun pientä venhoain	my little boat
Että murhe kauas	so that sorrow
	flees
poistuisi rinnastain	far away from
	my heart
Tuudittele tuonne	Rock gently
missä myrsky käy	where the storms
	are raging
Missä aallot pauhaa	where the waves
	are rolling
eikä maata näy.	and no land is in
	sight.

At an agreed sign, we rocked the boat quite hard. We kept repeating it every once in a while, and finally Elina said, "Because you kids simply cannot behave yourselves, you better go back to the shore." They rowed towards the shore, singing:

Ei se ole raukka,	A poor little soul
	is not he who
joka rantoja soutaa,	is rowing near
	the shoreline
rantoja soutaa	rowing near the
	shoreline
Vaan se on raukka,	A poor little soul
	is he who

72

joka rannalla istuu,	is sitting on the shore
rannalla istuu	sitting on the shore
ja itkee.	and weeping.

I did not like Master Aleksi as much as I had liked Uncle Lönroos. It was not that Master Aleksi was not a very friendly and pleasant person. He asked me to come and see his apple orchard. He had planted three hundred trees in the spring, and with pride he told me that not a single one had died. Then we went to see the long, beautiful beds of strawberries, between which young boys were pulling out weeds. The boys had come from the village to ask for such work, having heard that the Master of the Manor paid good wages to all his laborers. Now he told me to stop and wait a while, then he shouted to the boys, "That's quite enough for today. Come again tomorrow." And he gave each boy some money from his pocket. The boys thanked him and took off, running. After the boys had gone, we went to see the beehives. They sat under the apple tree in long orderly rows. And he said to me, "Anni, don't come here during the day, the bees don't like strangers, but at night like this they are calm." When we started back towards the manor, I mustered my courage and asked, did he not like his job as the manager of the paper mill? He said he had only been there to please his father, because his father had always wanted his son to inherit the paper mill. But as for himself, he said that even as a young man he had wanted to own land, and now that his father was dead, he had made his wish come true.

At midsummer, a large "evangelical meeting"

was held at the manor. Many speakers and priests arrived to preach at the meeting. Lots of people came, even from farther-away towns and villages, forming an enormous congregation. Many Finns still remember how these meetings took place in towns and villages, how many fervent preachers explained religious teachings to devout listeners, and how every now and then the great sound of the singing crowd would carry even into people's houses. Aunt Linda was an outstanding hostess, organizing plenty of food for this large gathering. There were even great cauldrons of raisin soup, made in the servants' kitchens. And it tasted good. Many people came to thank Aunt Linda for her unusual soup. I saw an elderly man come to see Aunt Linda, saying, "I've tasted soup made by many a madam, but this was by far the best I've ever eaten". Then again, I noticed that Aunt Linda had not been stingy with the ingredients. But before the meeting ended, heavy rains started, and Aunt Linda was wondering whatever to do with the rest of the food, seeing as people left and went home. It sure was real "Hay Days" for the farmhands and maids, having such good food for a few days. Yet there was so much that the rest went bad and had to be given to the pigs.

Soon after that it was time to celebrate Aunt Linda's birthday. On the previous day, the summer guests from Helsinki were singing together, and they asked me which spiritual song was Aunt's favorite song, so they could serenade her with it, I said it was from the "The Zither of Zion". On the morning of Aunt Linda's birthday, we got up at 5 AM and sang beneath her window:

Autuus suuri	Great bliss,
oomme Herran kansa	we are people of the Lord
Vahv' on sanassa se todistus	Powerful is that testimony in the Word
Kiitos, kiitos,	Thank you, thank you
rakkaudestansa	for the love
jonka liekis' ompi uudistus.	whose flame brings renewal

Aunt Linda got up, opened the window and thanked the ad hoc choir for waking her up so beautifully early in the morning.

One day I mentioned to Aunt Linda that in the autumn, I was planning to return to the city that I had had to leave four years ago when my Father's great hopes had been crushed to pieces. My Father wanted me to continue my studies there, but Aunt did not agree. She said she would write at once to my Father in America and ask him whether I could stay on, as her foster daughter. Aunt and I waited for his reply with great anticipation. When Father wrote back, he said that my staying on with Aunt Linda was out of the question, as apparently Aunt Linda did not get along with the children of her husband, Master Aleksi. They had left home as soon as Aunt and Master Aleksi had married. Toimi, the eldest of Master Aleksi's children, was staying at the manor for the summer, but he had a job in Helsinki and he would go back there in the autumn. So Father wanted me to go to school in the city, and live in a boarding house. Aunt was sad about my leaving, saying we would have had such a nice time together. True, I did know how to behave so that Aunt would be pleased, and see to her guests exactly according to her wishes. As I was saying my good-byes to Master Aleksi and Aunt Linda, she gave me a copy of "The Zither of Zion" (a hymnal) as well as a copy of "A stranger's life at home" (a prayer book), insisting that I come back at once if I did not like going to school in the city.

(To be continued)

Episode 13, 13 Aug 1954

Many changes had taken place in the city during my absence. The first person I met was my childhood friend Hilda, who, during my first school years, so often entertained us with her skillful drawings when we had to spend our nights with her while our parents were at evangelical meetings. Now Hilda wanted me to come and live with her and her mother. Her twin brothers had already gone to America, so young. Hilda's mother had a shop booth at the market place, and a young girl was working there. Hilda still went to the Ateneum, and by now she had become quite accomplished at drawing and painting, she had sold several pieces already. She told me very openly about her life. She had found herself a friend. In those days, the "Guards Battalion" was based in Helsinki. It was the General Governor's life guard's battalion. Handsome young men were picked for it, all of equal height. Hilda's friend was in the Guards, a young man named Toivo, Hilda told me that they had already exchanged eternal vows and decided to marry when Toivo's military service ended.

76

His home was somewhere in the countryside, in the Uusimaa province. I did not start school that autumn, but worked as Hilda and her mother's housekeeper.

Then the time came for Toivo to be discharged from the Guard, and Hilda and I went to the square to see the guardsmen's last parade. The band was playing:

Pojat kansan urhokkaat,

mi Puolan, Lütz, Leipzigin

tantereilla verta vuoti.

Viel' on Suomi voimissaan,

voi vihollisen hurmehella

peittää maan.

You sons of our brave people who shed your blood on the battle fields of Poland, Lytzen, Leipzig and Narva Finland is still powerful, with the enemy's blood she will cover the land.

With tears in her eyes, Hilda waved as Toivo marched by. That night, Toivo came to see Hilda, and when he was leaving, he promised to write often. He said he would not stay at home for too long, he would come back to town soon.

So Hilda had to console herself with just Toivo's letters. A couple of letters did arrive, and Hilda was so happy, so hopeful. Then one morning, when Hilda had gone to the Ateneum, the mail arrived and I brought it in. Hilda's mother was still at home, and she went through the mail and found a letter addressed to

Hilda. It was from Toivo. She opened it, read it, and put it in the stove, so it burned in the fire, and she strictly forbade me to ever to mention a single word of it to anyone. As an aside she said, "That Toivo is not worthy of Hilda."

Ever since that morning Hilda's mother made sure that she was the first person to get hold of the day's mail. I noticed that Hilda grew very sad and she no longer spoke of Toivo. I was so childish that I did not dare tell Hilda what had happened to the letters sent to her. I was afraid of Hilda's mother. In my heart I felt great pity for poor Hilda, for she must have believed that Toivo had betrayed her. I was thinking that there was a very fitting song, sung by a young girl to her mother:

Kuules, mun kulta äitini,	Oh, my dear mother, listen to me
Kuule mun rukoukseni;	please hear my prayer
Huojenna sa huoleni	Relieve my worries
ja huokaukseni.	and my sighs.

But the reply would not have fit in the mouth of this mean mother:

Jos tehdä lemmen tietäisin	If I knew how to conjure up love
Kyll' ainoon lapsein auttaisin	surely I would help my only child
Surut hältä suistaisin	Remove her

78

	sorrows
ja huolet poistaisin.	and chase away her worries.

After a while I noticed that Hilda had found new friends, but there was no one special. They were "only" friends from school and work that she invited to spend evenings with us. They were young men and women who had the same ideas and pastimes as Hilda herself. Often they would discuss the models they had been painting. Once, an elderly man had posed for them. He was quite a bit under the influence of alcohol and yet he was capable of standing and posing for them for an hour. They were laughing, who cared if he was so badly "influenced", he had a suitably shaped body and that was the only thing that mattered. Back at home, Hilda had used me as a model, and she had produced some quite nice "portraits". When her friends saw them, they asked me would I come and pose at the Ateneum, it would pay one mark per hour. Well, of course one mark per hour would have been good, but I could never ever have posed for a roomful of painters.

Hilda was at home on washing days, and then we always had a good time. The laundry was separate from the main building, and no sound carried from there to the house, so we could sing to our hearts' content, and we sure remembered well every possible love song there was.

Even Hilda lightened up when we sang:

He istuivat illan tullen	As evening came, they were

	sitting
lähtehen reunalla.	by a spring.
Huokaus siinä	A sigh
sotilaan rinnasta kohosi	burst forth from
	the soldier's
	breast
Hän morsiantaan syleili	He embraced his
	fiancée
ja sanoin kuiskasi.	and spoke to her
	in whisper.

And when we were done with that long song,
she began another one:

Yksi kauppias Intiasta	There was a
	merchant from
	India
rikas ja ylhäinen	rich and high-
	born
Hänellä oli tytär	He had a
	daughter
Maria niminen.	called Maria.

Or this one:

Kukkaisten keskellä	Amidst flowers
kukkulalla	on a hill
nyt Hjalmari lauleskeli Hjalmari	was singing
Menneistä ajoista	of times gone by,
muinaisista	times ancient
siin' yksin vain	All alone
muistutteli.	he was
	reminiscing

She even sang this song from beginning to end:

Pohjois-Amerikassa	In North America
Philadelphian kaupungissa	in the town of Philadelphia
oli neito Maria nimeltä	there lived a maiden called Maria
ja sisarensa Liisa.	and her sister Liisa.

In that way, Hilda was trying to forget her sorrow and bitterness for her belief that she had been let down. Once, when Alma, the servant girl and I, were almost done with all laundry, Hilda said that in the past week, at a soirée, she had learned a completely new song, asking whether we would like hear it. Well of course, we said at once. So she sang:

Sandor oli kunnon sotamies ennen,	Sandor used to be a good soldier
kunnes kultans' hylkäs,	until he left his loved one
luotaan pois mennen.	and went away.
Palfy Istvan riisti hältä pois kullan,	Palfy Istvan took his loved one,
kuula Palfyn peitti hänet Palfy's alle mullan.	a bullet sent him six feet under.

I thought that very clearly Hilda was still thinking of her soldier boy, seeing as how often she sang about soldiers.

Hilda's mother had to work in the shop alone all

day when Alma was doing the laundry, but I could not feel the slightest shred of pity for her. She had divorced from her drunk of a husband when their children were very young, and she had raised them alone, with great industry, which was probably why she considered it her privilege to decide whom Hilda should be allowed to marry. Every now and then, Hilda's father tried to come and see them, but only when he was well and truly drunk. Thus it was customary to always keep the doors locked, so he could not just march in, uninvited. One night, when we were all sitting and reading some magazine, there was the loudest knock on the door. Hilda's mother jumped up and tried to peer through the door window, but she could not see anything.

(To be continued)

Episode 14, 17 Aug 1954

Whispering, Hilda told her mother not to open the door, just ask who it is. But before she asked, there was another knock, even louder, and a rough man's voice shouted: "Open the door. It's death come knocking here." Hilda said, it is Father, drunk again. We were quiet, but all sorts of terrible threats kept coming from outside. Hilda's mother said, "Anni, you must run and get the police." She saw that the man had gone to the front steps and stopped his ranting and raving for a moment. She opened the door quickly, pushed me out and re-locked the door. With my heart in my throat I ran past the drunken man, out to the street. Soon the same loud racket started again. The man had gone back to the door.

I ran so hard that I felt fit to burst, and found a police constable at the street corner. I had to catch my breath before I could explain why I was there. The policeman patted my shoulder, and said, "Don't you worry, little girl, we will lock that fool up in no time." We walked briskly to the house, and still that voice was yelling those same threats. I do not know why the policeman told me to go first, and I was going to refuse, but he said I needed not be afraid. When the man saw the police constable behind me, the stream of threats came to a sudden stop. The policeman took him away, and the next day we received the summons to the local court of justice. It was the first time I saw a Finnish courthouse, and the last.

It was absolutely terrifying. I was frightened as I sat on the bench in that big courthouse, waiting for my turn. I tried to recall what my Father had told me about the questions he had been asked during a court session. Suppose I had to say: "Yes Your Honor" or "High Justice", or something like that. When they finally called me in and asked whether I was the Miss Anni Södergren who had called the police, I tried to be very brave, though my knees were trembling, and I said: "Yes Your Honor." Then the judge simply smiled at me kindly and asked me my age. I told him my age, and he said that was all, I could go. And just to think how I spent the previous night wide awake, worried about how I should behave, how I would tell the truth, then endure all sorts of cross-examination. And then all the dreadful tension and fears were relieved as easy as that. Nevertheless, now I had been to court. A poem I had recited in school came to mind:

Ah kellä puhdas tunto on	Ah, he whose conscience is clearing
ja laittamaton kieli	whose tongue does not lie
jot' oikeast ei horjuttaa,	who cannot be distracted from what is right
ei väärän puoleen johdattaa	nor led astray to what is wrong
voi vilpin viehätykset	by attractions of insincerity.
Sen silmä aina kirkas on	His eyes are always bright
ja otsa puhdas hohtaa	his forehead pure and shinning
poves' on sydän pelvoton	his heart fearless in his chest
jos kuinka kumman khotaa	on matters that he should encounter.

I reckon the poem was only fitting for grownups, because at least I had been very much afraid.

Then, one day, a middle-aged, kind-looking man came to our house. He said he had seen me at the court house and asked, would I come and help them with housekeeping, for pay. I was ever so delighted, and ready to go at once. I wrote to my Father, telling him that I had not started school after all, but taken a housekeeping job instead, and I would stay there until he sent me a ticket so that I too could go to America.

My job was with a small family, taking care of two children. Other housekeeping duties were done by a very dried-up looking spinster, for whom I had to make coffee in the morning. She would have seven cups of coffee in one go, before she would do anything else. The mistress noticed it and considered such coffee drinking a bit too much, wondering what to do. Then she thought of a good way to handle it. She said, "Anni, you run to the store and get some chicory. Put a big chunk in the coffee pot and only half as much coffee as you've used so far."

All went well, and the spinster kept drinking and drinking coffee, as always. But one day she went to get something from the cupboard, and she found the chicory that I foolishly enough had not thought of hiding. She flew into a right hissy fit and blamed it all on me, saying, "Anni, you cheeky little monkey, what a naughty trick you've played on me". I did not dare utter a single word, but finally the mistress got her to calm down. The chicory was tossed in the rubbish, and the housekeeper's coffee drinking continued as before.

On my nights off I sometimes went to see Hilda. On those nights she invited other young people too, so of course we sang a lot. We sang many folksongs, such as this one:

Sä kasvoit neito kaunoinen	Pretty maiden, you grew up
isäsi majassa,	in your father's house
kuin kukka kaunis, suloinen,	like a flower, beautiful and sweet

vihreellä nurmella.	in the green grass.

Or, this one:

Yksi ruusu on kasvanut	A single rose grew
laaksossa,	in the valley
ja niin kauniisti kukoistaa.	and it blossoms so beautifully.
Yksi kulkijapoika on nähnyt sen	A wanderer boy saw it
eikä voi sitä unhoittaa.	and cannot forget it.

Hilda always had in store for us a new song that we had not heard before. This time she said, "I have a song in the dialect of Karelia, and it is a love song. But before singing the song, I'm going to serve my guests coffee". After the coffee, she began:

Usiast' tulloop miull	Often comes into my mind
aika se ettee,	the time
ku pirttin uutee	when into a new home
mie kullan toin.	I brought my loved one.
Annoi avaimet kullan kättee	I gave the keys in the hands of my love
ja huilut iloiset vastaan soi.	and merry flutes welcomed us.
Katos orretki uuvet kiilsit	New beams

86

ja kulta

puuhais' naurus suin.

Silt' se tuntu siin ku silmäel'

jot' mu kottii kaik' kaunistui.

were shining in the ceiling and my loved one bustled about, laughing. Seeing it, it seemed as if everything in my home had became more beautiful.

When she had sung the other verses and was singing the last verse:

Lemmen liekki kans'

usiast sammuup
Rakkaus kauniskin.

katoo pois.
Silloin syömmen sisuspuol

tummuup.

Often the flame of love may also go out Even the most beautiful love may fade away Then the inside of one's heart grows dark.

There her voice suddenly broke, and she burst into tears, poor Hilda.

The next time I went to see her, she was not at home. I was going to leave as soon as I had come, but Hilda's mother was at home and she said to me, "Why don't you sit down for a moment, and let's have a chat." She said, 'Now Hilda has a fiancé. He is a professor at a school, a well respected gentleman, though quite a bit older than Hilda. I am ever so pleased that I broke it off between Hilda and Toivo in time. Now Hilda will be counted among the better people, instead of her having had to become just a country wife. I listened to Hilda's mother without saying a word, but I was thinking to myself, surely Hilda's mother had her fingers in this pie, too. Then I said good-bye and asked her to give Hilda my regards.

Around then, I met Aunt Linda's stepson, Master Aleksi's eldest son Toimi, and we had such a good time, and much to talk about. Laughing, we reminisced how, back at his father's manor, we had had so much fun, and how we had teased Elina and "Foudi" in the boat and they had called us "brats". We felt that we had grown up quite a bit since those summer days. Toimi would often come by on weekends and take me out to concerts of vocal or instrumental music. I recall a particular concert, where they performed instrumental music by Finnish and foreign master composers. Those pieces were such high art that no one understood them more than that countryman who listened to a symphony for a while, then asked: "When are they going to be done practicing so they can start playing?"

However, at the end of the program, they played several pieces of music that everyone could understand. To our astonishment, their final number was:

Eikä ne pienet linjaalirattaat	The small horse carriage does not
keinutella kestä ja kestä;	take a lot of

eikä se vanha uudelle kullalle

menemästä estä, ja estä."

rocking and
rocking
nor does an old
love stop one
from
going to a new
one

(To be continued)

Episode 15, 20 Aug 1954

Then I told Toimi how in that summer I had had an adventure and ended up a witness in the local court. Toimi asked, did you remember to say "Yes, your honor", or "Yes, high court". Well of course I had not remembered, having been so frightened that I hardly remembered anything at all, barely able to stammer my name, even though I had spent most of the night awake, thinking about my upcoming court appearance. Toimi was amused by my story, and as it ended he said, "Were you not disappointed to get off so lightly. All you had to do was answer a single question, when you imagined that you had become involved in such a court case that it would be something to tell about even to your grandchildren."

Again, strange news was making rounds of the workings of Governor General Bobrikoff and the Russification of Finland. A grand statue had been built in front of the Old Church to commemorate the great Finnish poet and author Topelius. It was supposed to be unveiled in a grand ceremony, but then an order from Bobrikoff arrived, forbidding speeches and ceremonies at the unveiling. Late that night, we too went to see the statue. There were lots of flowers around it. (At this point Antti interrupted his mother Anni Ahola's story, asking, "Are you now talking about the statue in that picture in your 'scrapbook', with Väinämöinen and his zither? And that woman, is it Aino or does that woman mean Finland? And there are lots of flowers in that picture.")

"That's the very statue; I managed to get the picture just before I came to this country, and I have kept it so I can show it to my children and grandchildren. I value this picture very highly, for even though I am a two-hundred-percent American, I am still a tull-blooded Finn. (I will tell more about being two-hundred-percent American later, when it is time for it.)

The Finnish people grew increasingly harassed under the tyranny of Bobrikoff, and so the members of a particular association decided to put an end to it. They drew lots to decide which of them would sacrifice his life on the altar of the freedom of Finland. The members of this association were young graduate students, and the lot fell to Eugen Schauman, who, as is well known, shot first Bobrikoff, then himself.

When Eugen's body was taken to the mortuary, people wanted to come and view it, but Russian gendarmes watching the building drove everybody off. Then a group of us youngsters decided to get some flowers and we tossed them over the wall to the mortuary, but as soon as any flowers crossed the wall, a Russian gendarme was there, stamping the flowers, but we did not let up, instead as soon as some of us had tossed the flowers over the wall, others came and brought more, and finally there were too many flowers

90

for the gendarme to destroy completely.

Eugen was buried in secrecy, at night, outside the city, on the orders of the Russian high command, and no marker was put up on his grave. Every full-blown patriot was hoping that this young man had not had to sacrifice his life in vain. The next Governor General did turn out to be more conciliatory.

A ticket and travel money arrived from my Father in America. I went to see Hilda, to tell her that now it was my turn to leave for the golden land in the west. She was ever so kind, she told me to leave my job at once and to come and stay with them and make my travel preparations there, and she promised to help me with them. I was going to take with me as little as possible, so I decided to sell my precious library, of whose diversity I had been so proud. Books are so heavy and bulky to transport. I left behind The Kalevala and all other award books, except for the bible I had received at school, I did not have the heart to leave it, remembering how I had carried it to my late mother's hands. And of course I had to take that large pictorial bible which my Father had so painstakingly compiled from the "village library magazine". I was preparing for an unknown future, like this:

Kuin aalto aavalla merellä	Like a wave on the high seas
on tuuliajolla	is adrift in the winds
Niin ihmisenkin elämä	So is the life of a human being
on maailman matkoilla.	in the travels of the world

One night, Hilda and I sat sewing the very last piece of clothing to be put in my travel trunk. Hilda seemed completely lost in her own thoughts which I did not dare disturb, even though I so much wanted to ask whether she had heard anything from Toivo. Instead, I started to hum quietly:

Amanda käveli ryytimaassa	Amanda was walking amidst herbs
kukkasia poimimassa.	picking flowers.
Hän poimi Hermannille kukkia	She was picking flowers for Hermanni
vaan Hermannia ei kuulukaan.	but Hermanni seems not to be coming.

I finally broke the silence between us and said to Hilda, "Would you go if you were in my place?" Startled, she came up from her dream world, asking, "Anni, what did you say?" "I was just asking that if you were in my place, would you go to America?"

It was not that I did not want to study further, but I kept thinking about those long, lonely winter nights at a "boarding house" without a real home, without Father or Mother. I wrote to Father that I did not wish to stay here by myself for a long time. You do remember that Father has been there for a year now? Many others have gone, and so I suppose I am going to go, too, be it wise or stupid, but now I neither can nor want to back out of it.

What neither of us almost did not believe at all,

was when Hilda's mother said she would be going on the same boat. "Well, my, oh my goodness" said Hilda, completely dumbfounded. But Hilda's mother said, it was really perfectly natural, seeing as how her twin sons were in America. So, of course as their mother she wanted to go to them. But Hilda and I winked at each other, knowing full well the reason for her departure. And we reckoned that it was not such a sudden decision after all, because soon after my Mother's death we had noticed that Hilda's mother would not have minded becoming my Father's new wife. Of course she had been planning the trip to America for quite a while, because she already had a buyer lined up for her store, and all she needed to do was to give some final instructions to Hilda.

I hoped that the "nasty old bag" would have gone sooner, so perhaps Hilda would have been reunited with her Toivo. But no, Hilda's mother made sure that the banns were read for Hilda and the man she had picked for her, and that they tied the marital knot soon after. Still, I knew full well what Hilda was thinking about Toivo:

En voi sua unhoittaa poies	I can never forget you,
vaikk'en ikänä sua saa.	though I can never have you.
Sä sydämessäni olet	In my heart you will stay
ikuisessa muistossa.	forever in my memories.

(To be continued)

93

Episode 16, 24 Aug 1954

Suddenly, time seemed to fly as if it had wings. That week, I met many school-time friends. They all wished me all the best, when I told them that I was going, and I even met one of the teachers. Aunt Linda came to town, too, asking me to give her regards to Uncle Lönroos, if I happened to meet him. On the day of the departure, Toimi Arnio came to the harbor with a large bouquet of flowers, and his last words were some broad hints of first love and of staying true, and while we had talked about all possible political and otherwise topical issues when we had spent time together, there had never been a single word of love, so at the moment of my departure, and thus our parting, it seemed altogether funny and ridiculous.

Lots of young people were going, and leaving their beloved country of birth, perhaps for ever. They were still happy to get away from under the Russian tyranny, yet they could not help thinking with regret of those who stayed behind.

Me riennämme Suomen rannoilta,	We hasten away from the shores of Finland,
maan rakkahan, kalliin kunnailta.	from the hills of the beloved, precious land.

During the trip, lots of new acquaintances were made, and many of us turned out to have the same destinations in America. All the time, familiar songs were resounding in the air, such as this one:

94

Sini-aaltosia pitkin,	On blue waves
alus uljas keinuaa	a proud ship is sailing
Lännen rusko purppurainen	Purple skies in the west
päivän tuloa ennustaa.	herald a new day.

On the deck, young people were dancing in a whirl of motion, and there was no shortage of music, because several young men had brought music instruments, and they took turns playing them. I saw a young man sitting apart from the others. As if only to himself, he was quietly playing on the fiddle the melody to this song:

Pium, paum, kannel kajahtaa,	Bing, bong, the zither resounds
ja nuoret karkelohon kiiruhtaa.	and the young rush to the dance floor
Pium, paum, viulu vingahtaa,	Bing, bong, the fiddle plays
ja joukko tanssissa jo tanhuaa.	and the young are dancing.

I was not keen on dancing. Instead I liked to walk around the decks. It occurred to me that I ought to go to the stern, so perhaps I might see that compass, as in that song:

| Oli kuutamo-ilta kaunis | It was a beautiful moonlit night |

Atlantin merellä	on the Atlantic Ocean
laivamme kulki hiljaa,	Our ship was sailing smoothly
keinuen aalloilla.	rolling with the waves.
Minä vahdissa seisoin,	I was standing watch,
kompassia katselin.	looking at the compass.
Sen neula pohjoista näytti,	Its needle was pointing north
joss' on mun armaani.	where my loved one lives.

In England, we had to wait for a couple of days for the ship that would sail across the Atlantic, and all passengers were inspected. The officials wanted to know whether the passengers had been vaccinated. Those who did not have a vaccination mark on their arm were vaccinated. One official took special notice of me, and it was making me wonder, what on earth does it mean? He could clearly see the vaccination mark on my arm, but then he was staring at my hair which was auburn and braided into two long braids. I was happy that Hilda had tied the braids off with beautiful silk ribbons. When my inspection turn ended, the official did not let me go with the others, instead he took me by the hand, then he took me to another room where there were several official-looking people seated at the tables. He said something to them that of course I did not understand. Then he returned to the room from which he had brought me.

A couple of men stood up and came to me.

They took the silk ribbons off my braids. Then they unfastened my thick braids until my hair was all loose. They babbled an awful lot. I tried to memorize their words, thinking I would look them up in a dictionary I had with me. Goodness how afraid I was, but then the men began to laugh. The man holding my ribbons gave them back to me, patted me kindly on the shoulder, opened the door and led me back to the others. They gathered around me, asking what had been done to me, and when I explained what had happened, we all came to the conclusion that since I had such an unusually thick and long hair, the officials must have thought it was fake, and I was a "smuggler", carrying something illegal, maybe opium, cocaine, or something else. I studied my dictionary but failed to come to any satisfactory conclusion. So I decided that the officials must have thought that I had fake braids and that I was carrying whatever contraband within them.

In England, the meals were so heavily seasoned with pepper that we Finns did not find it to our liking at all. But the bread was white and tasty, so that a countryman from Northern Finland thought it was just "coffee bread". When he was coming out of the dining room, he said to us, "Go thru' that door there, and you'll get to eat all the 'nisu' you could possibly want."

The trip across the Atlantic passed quickly, because I did not suffer from sea sickness at all, and the seamen paid special attention to me, a young slip of a girl. They made me a swing from ropes, and every now and then they would send me swinging high with a hefty push. Even the ship's chef came to see me several times, bringing me sweet pastries wrapped in paper napkins on several days.

Hilda's mother was awfully sea-sick, so when I told her about the sweet pastries, she was horrified and said, "You better toss those pastries into the ocean, God knows what they are feeding you". But I did not see why I should be so mistrustful, so I just ate the pastries and they were really ever so good.

The young Finnish travelers kept flocking together, waiting to see the shores of America, and if they were not dancing, they were singing, for instance:

Ylös nuorten parvi sankka

Stand up, all you young people

missä kansan toiveet on.

wherein the hopes of the nation lie

Ylös Suomen suoja vankka

Stand up, Finland's sturdy shield,

nouse työhön, taisteloon.

stand up to work, or to fight

Ollos valon valpas vahti,

Be the alert guardians of the light

etsi syväin syntyin mahti,

find the power of your ancestors

avosilmin seiso vaan.

stand up, with your eyes wide open.

On the sea, it was easy to see that the world is round: when one saw ships on the high seas, at first one could see just the tips of their masts. Then little by little one could see more and more, as they came closer. Soon we were in the western hemisphere. Before leave-taking, those who had become friends exchanged addresses, promising to visit, if it was possible in a new land and in new circumstances, where, as the song says:

Ei tarvitse herroja palvella,

eikä niitä kumartaa
vaan niinkuin omalle veljelleen

saa asiansa toimittaa.

You need neither serve the masters nor bow to them but as if with your own brother you may deal with them.

Sure, if one can manage the language, I would like to add, because that is the very first difficulty an emigrant encounters after arriving here. In Canada, our ship docked at Quebec. Most travelers had to go on by train, but my ticket was to Montreal, along with three other passengers. Hilda's mother was among the former group. The four of us headed for Montreal had another stopover, but just overnight. In the morning, a westbound train would leave to cross the continent. We had to spend the night in the large hall at the railway station. The night fell, and everyone else was settling on the long benches on one side of the hall, but on the other side, I was sitting alone, thinking. After a while, the only sound I could hear was that of even snoring. Exhausted, the travelers had fallen

100

asleep.

(To be continued)

Episode 17, 27 Aug 1954

I, too, settled on my bench, though I was not going to sleep. Then I saw two men wearing dark masks enter the hall very quietly. At first I did not see them clearly because the hall attendent had switched off the lights much earlier. One of them had a flash light in his hand, and they were creeping towards me. I kept my eyes shut and pretended to sleep. Very carefully, the men took another long bench and set it next to mine, with its back towards the room, forming a sort of a bed. Then one man began to go through my pockets, while the other was shining the light on me. (In those days, it was the European fashion for dresses to have pockets.) But I did not have any money in any of the pockets. I had hidden my money elsewhere, but of course the men could not know that, and it seemed that they had been emptying emigrants' pockets before. I tried to figure out the smartest thing for me to do, I did not dare scream, because the man holding the flash light seemed to have a revolver in his other hand, and if I screamed, he might shoot. Suddenly I remembered a good gymnastics move that I had performed especially well at school. So, in the blink of an eye, I jumped to my feet and stood up on the bench, then, just as quickly, I jumped over the back and landed on the floor with an almighty thump. The men must have been startled, because quickly they switched off their flash light, and ran out.

The thump woke up my fellow travelers, and sleepily they began to inquire, what on earth was that noise? When I told them about my adventure, they were mad at me for not calling for help. I said I had been afraid of the revolver and thought that I would sort out the situation on my own, which I had done. Had I screamed, I might just have ended up a target for their bullets, and then perhaps I would never see this wonderful land.

The journey inland was rather dull, and the towns we passed seemed dirty and miserable, quite unclean in comparison with the beautiful towns in Finland. But, upon arrival at my destination, the joy of reunion made me forget all the trouble of traveling. Oh, Father, Father! I am still your little daughter, aren't I? A year's separation from you was unbearably long, but now it seemed a bygone dream, not worth reminiscing. My heart felt as if bursting with joy, I wanted to sing, to laugh, to do all things at once. For a while, we talked of this and that. Then Father turned very serious. He gave me a picture; the photograph of a young woman, and said, "This is my wife. I hope you will become good friends." "So do I, and congratulations to you", I managed to say, barely.

My Father was living in a large beach town, with a very nice young couple. They had a sweet little boy who reminded me a lot of the little boy I had taken care of in Helsinki just before leaving for America. These young people were Finnish, and they introduced me to their friends, and often, to my delight, the mistress took me with her when she went visiting, and so while I was living with them, I was never homesick for Finland, that struck me later.

My Father was working at a shipyard, earning $1.92 a day, which was good money at the time. He told me that he had already been given land (a homestead) by the government to live on, and that after five years of living and farming the homestead becomes the property of its settler. Right after landing, he had also filed the first "land record", and so the full record would be filed five years later.

My Father's new wife was already in the countryside, staying with her sister, and in the autumn we would go there, too. My Father had many good friends here, although he had not been here for long. It was probably because in Finland he had been a businessman, and because he had the kind of personality that he made friends easily, and he never ran out of good stories.

I remember how once, in Finland, when my Mother was still alive, a young woman came to visit us. She did not tell us her name, and Mother did not ask, she just kindly told her to take a seat, and made her coffee. The visitor was looking around the room, and she saw a large picture of Father on the wall. She looked at it very closely for a moment and then she said to Mother: "That is your son, isn't it?" Mother said, "It is my husband". Then the visitor suddenly turned very pale, and she said that she had gotten a bad tooth ache, and she left in a hurry. Afterwards we learned that the young woman had taken my Father's funny stories at face value, and she had come to see my Father's "mother".

On Sundays, we would visit my Father's friends. Everyone was ever so friendly, but I later heard that they had found me haughty, for speaking with such a

Helsinki-dweller's accent. Of course it never occurred to them that at the time, it was the only way I knew how to speak (but now I can speak Northern Finnish and Finglish, too).

PART IV: YOUTH IN AMERICA, EPISODES 17-36

What I liked best was listening to Father tell about the homestead where we would soon go and live. He said it was on the shores of a big, beautiful lake, and I imagined it much like the manor house of Master Aleksi and Aunt Linda back in Kauninki, Finland. I got a more realistic picture in my mind of my Father's farm when he told me that it was in a newly settled area where there were neither roads nor schools, but he believed firmly that as soon as people settled there, the government would soon build both.

One day I met one of my fellow travelers who was from Tampere. He touched the brim of his hat briefly in greeting. He had already become Americanized. In Finland, boys would always tip their cap in greeting. Here's a very well fitting song:

Amerikkaan kun matkustin	When I went to America, in my mouth
oli suussani suomenkieli.	the Finnish language resounded.
Mutta hetken täällä kun oleilin,	But it did not take very long
niin muuttui mieli ja kieli.	for my language and thoughts to change.
Mä "käpiksi" seinasin lakkini	My "lakki" soon became a "cap"
kaulahivini kaleriks' muutin.	my "kaulahihna" a "collar"
Pois heitin sarkatakkini	I threw away my "sarkatakki"

ja oortasin "sappa suutin".

and ordered a "Dinner Jacket".

Town life in America seemed somehow second-rate in comparison with the life in the beautiful capital of Finland, as nothing was new. In Finland, there were automobiles, too, and they did not exactly threaten the safety of the pedestrians here, either. However, I expected to see new things in the countryside and I could not wait to go there. Before we left for the countryside, I met again my fellow traveler Tauno. He said he was going to Dakota and he promised to write to me often. Thinking about Tauno, this straight-backed Finnish sports star, my thoughts wandered far ahead, into the future. I remembered the many medals and "trophies" that he had won in the ranks of the sports club of Tampere. He would proudly show them to me and the other travelers. Now my thoughts were really beginning to take wings and fly, and I was thinking that perhaps Tauno and I would become special friends and perhaps one day he would return to this state, because of me. Quietly, I hummed to myself:

Eipä valkene konsaan päivä

Never shall such a day dawn

etten sinua muistaisi.

that I would not think of you.

Aina sydämeni syvyydessä

In the depths of my heart

kuvasi kallis on säilyvä.

your precious face will always remain.

(To be continued)

108

Episode 18, 31 Aug 1954

But in the end such dreams did not gain much of a foothold in my young mind. I made new acquaintances almost every day. I formed an especially close friendship with a particular young couple. This friendship is one that has lasted my whole life. It is the kinship of the great Finnish people which, here, in a foreign land and foreign circumstances feels especially dear and precious.

Then, one autumn day, Father decided that we should leave for the countryside. The first leg of the trip was by train to a small nearby station. Then we had to go on by foot. One could barely call it a path, because a stranger would surely have lost his way, but Father just walked on, chattering happily, reckoning he had marked the path so well that he could not get lost. Twilight was starting to fall and we had not arrived yet, and then Father lost sight of the path. He looked around, saying he had put spots in the trees as marks with an axe, wondering how he could not find them now. He took some tree bark, put it at the end of a long stick and lit it. He told me to sit tight and wait. I was sure we would stay here in the woods, lost forever, and fall prey to wolves, when Father gave a shout and told me to come and join him. He had found the path again, and soon we arrived at his homestead and dwelling. Hardly ever was rest so welcome as then, after a long day's wandering in the American wilderness.

In the morning I found much to wonder at, looking around and seeing how uninhabited and wild the whole place looked, and I said to Father: "Why don't you clear this land, remove all rubbish, bushes, dried-up trees and branches, and leave only those beautiful, straight, living trees standing to grow, as back at Aunt Linda's in the Kanunki manor." Father just smiled and said, "Dear child, you cannot possibly understand just yet. But take a walk with me to the boundaries of my piece of land, and you'll see that such a large clearing job is only partly possible even in the whole lifetime of a human generation."

Then we went down to the lake. From logs, Father had made a raft that he propelled a little ways off the shore with a long pole. On the raft there was an old bucket and fishing equipment. He told me to sit down and wait. We would soon have enough fish for soup, because the wind was westerly and so the fish would be biting well. Soon enough he did catch a couple of fish. He put them in the bucket, and then I understood its purpose. He even got his feet all wet as the waves sloshed over the raft. Full of hope, he told me that more homesteaders were on their way here, and soon they would build a saw mill and then he would get planks for a boat.

He was even hoeing the ground, for a field, but a day's work of hoeing did not accomplish much. I was amazed at his great industriousness. To think that here was a Finnish businessman, a-hoeing. He had lost a lot of weight and his hands were almost calloused, but he kept on working. Looking at him, I remembered a part of this song:

Siinä se leipä lainehtii	There is the rolling grain field,
ja aallosta nousee kala.	and fish rising from the waves.
Ja se pelto on pieni	And the field is

ja tupanen
kun pienen linnun pesä.

small,
and the cottage
like a little bird's
nest.

(Father has been dead for a long time, but today, fifty-two years later, the homestead he started is now a beautiful farm.)

Then a cold winter settled in, and it seemed a miracle how it finally turned into spring. My Father's wife had come to the homestead in the autumn. She told me many stories about her home in Northern Finland, and they made interesting listening because I knew next to nothing about life in the Finnish countryside. Father had already acquired a couple of cows, because as soon as he had arrived at his homestead, he had started building a cowshed from round logs, using clay as filling between the logs, and roofing the cowshed with large tree bark shingles. His wife churned butter and did many other chores, just as she had done at home, back in Finland.

We often met Indian women and men on the quiet forest paths. In the spring, a couple of Indian women came to visit. They seemed very shy and spoke no language that we could understand. My Father's wife knew a few words of English because she had lived in town for a couple of years, but she did not understand the Indian women: of course they were speaking in their own language. However, we managed to get along by using hand signs. We served them coffee, and I think they thanked us as they left. A couple of weeks later they came again, and I was wondering why they came this time. I asked them to come in. The older woman unwrapped a small parcel that she had brought. She had some maple sugar for us. My Father told me that in early spring, the Indians make holes in the stems of maple trees and run sap into vats. Then they boil the sap until it turns into thick syrup, and as it cools down, it hardens into sugar.

Sad memories of my Mother's death were now beginning to fade, and so was my home-sickness. All Indians vanished from these areas. New neighbors, all of them Finnish, arrived to settle in the area. So far, nobody was setting up the kind of sawmill that my Father was hoping for. Instead, they put up workbenches on top of which they lifted logs, for a two-man sawing team to split. In that way they made thick planks for flooring, and for other building uses.

These settlers had a lot of enthusiasm. It was amusing to listen to them talk about boundaries of their homesteads. Some of them had settled on wrong properties, but with joint effort they managed to locate land corner marks left by the state land surveyors. They lived in hopes that roads and schools would be built for them in the near future.

My Father's wife and I became acquainted easily. She was still young and full of life, and we decided to call each other by our Christian names, as it is friendlier, and after all, my Father had hoped that we would become good friends. And we sure did have a lot fun during the short while that I lived there. But I could write a whole book on how stupid I still was, even though I thought myself so smart in those days. I could have cried again over my stupidity, as I had when I was a little girl and Mother found me tearing those blossoms off the apple trees.

Despite a lot of struggle and hardship, these

settlers built buildings and got what cattle they could afford. The cattle were left free to roam the woods, as it was not possible to fence pastures for them. They came home reasonably obediently by themselves, as they always get some fodder when they were led into the cowshed. Then on one cloudy day they did not seem to be coming home, so I went to get them. After a short while of walking I thought I heard familiar cowbells. I began to call them by their names, "Home, come home now, come Kukka, come Hertta, come Nuppa, come home now, come Ruusa, come Punikki, here, come home now!"

But then it started to rain. Raindrops made the leaves in the trees rustle, and I no longer heard the cowbells. Hopeless, I turned for home when I saw a beautiful tree full of small reddish fruit, and I stopped to pick and taste them.

(To be continued)

Episode 19, 3 Sep 1954

The fruit tasted good, and the pits inside them were similar to those in the "viskuna" or "luumu" fruit (prunes) back in Finland. I was happy to have found something new here in the wilderness. It was a wild plum tree. When I finally got back home, tired and annoyed at not having found the cows, everyone was terribly upset and worried. Father said he had thought that the Indians had captured me, and he had gone and asked the neighbors to take their guns and go out looking for me. The cows had come home ages ago, of course, they had heard my calls, but when I did not return with the cows, my Father had feared

113

the worst. He had told the neighbors that in case Anni returns while they are out looking for her, he will shoot twice so they know they can come home, but in case they find me, they must shoot twice.

In the autumn I decided to go to town and find a job, though I was very anxious about how I was going to manage, what with the foreign language feeling so strange that I could not tell one word from the another, when it was spoken fast. No sooner said than done, and soon Father was seeing me off at the little railway station. Now the path had seen more use, and one could not get lost any longer. I was traveling with just a small bundle of clothes, a notebook and a pencil. I had decided to figure out every English word whose meaning I would come to understand. Just as I was leaving, I remembered how the old-country boy sang as he was leaving his home:

En saanu mä matkalle mukaani	When I left home, I was not given
kapsäkkiä, rihkamoita.	a suitcase or other things.
En monia hyviä ohjeita	Neither did I get good advice
enkä helliä suuteloita.	nor tender kisses.

And so I started my "circulating school of the world". I went to the biggest city in Minnesota. There, some female relatives received me ever so kindly. They helped me so much, starting by providing me with all necessary clothing. I wrote down every sum of money they spent on my behalf, with the firm intention that as soon as I had a job, I would pay all of it back.

114

The English language turned out not to be so difficult after all, once I got started. I soon learned the words for the various kind of foodstuff, but, written down, they were so entirely different that I wrote down each word as I heard them pronounced, in the way the Finnish language works. Thus a funny thing happened when I was going to a store with my cousin. On a wall I saw a big sign: "Butter nut bread". I asked, "Why does that sign say butter, but not bread?" My cousin burst into merry gales of laughing. She said that I seemed to understand some words, but not quite right. She told me that the sign said "butter nut bread". I had thought "nut" was "not". My cousin said, "Anni, you will get the hang of it soon."

Of course it would have been easy to get a job if I had had the least bit of experience. I was happy when I got a job with a small family, and I could start using the notes I had made of the words I had learned. I did not show my language book to anyone, but as soon as I found out how a given word was written, I wrote it down on the line I had reserved for it. I did not know my way around in this big city, except to where my relatives lived, so I had plenty of time to study, and it was like a school to me. In this household, the master was the first to get up in the morning, and when I went into the kitchen, he was already lighting a fire in the stove. And, oh "Abba dear Father" how that man would talk all the time, and I did not understand a single word. Such prattle seemed ever so funny to me, but what do you know, three months later I was able to use everyday words and speak of daily things quite passably myself. Then I left this job and went to an employment office to get a different job, and they sent me to another town, in another state. Now I had a job in a large hotel and I arrived late at night. Early in the morning I went into the kitchen and was ready to start dish washing, wearing a new apron. After a while, people began to arrive. One woman started to make coffee. Then a formal looking woman walked in, and I guessed that she was the matron. She came to me and asked why I was standing next to the dish washing sink.

I answered: "The employment office sent me here for a dishwasher's job, but I don't know how and I want to learn." She said that she did not need a dishwasher, and just then a brisk young girl walked in and, looking sure of her position, went straight to the dish washing sink, from which I had distanced myself a little. I lost all hope and started taking off my apron, telling the matron, "Then I must leave now."

The matron said: "Wait a moment, young girl; would you like to learn to cook food? I need another cook." "Of course I want to learn," I said. Then she asked how old I was. With a perfectly straight face, I said eighteen, though I had just turned fifteen when I left my Father's farm. The matron did not doubt my words, as I was big for my age, and my cousins had taught me to set my hair in the "grown-up" fashion of those days. Soon it was midday, and I asked the dishwasher girl if she would be so good as to tell me where I could find a bookstore. She did, and I rushed there and asked to buy the biggest cookbook they had.

So I began my second subject in the "circulating school of the world". I read my book every night, while the other girls went out. Nobody else spoke Finnish here. We were a dozen young girls working there, and the third floor of the building was

116

appointed as our accommodation. Sometimes such home sickness would overwhelm me that not even those "studies" helped me pass time, and from memory I would recite this beautiful poem over and over again:

Oi synnyinmaa

Oh, land of my birth

sun sankar'muistoissasi

your heroic memories

mun liikkuu aatokseni ainiaan.

are forever in my thoughts.

Suurtöitäs lemmin;

I treasure your great deeds,

muistan mainettasi

I remember your fame,

Ja niihin tunteineni uppoan.

with all my feelings, I sink myself in them.

En pyydä maailma

Oh, world, I do not ask for

loistoo, riemuasi,

your glories or your joys,

pois onni elonikin kadotkoon.

let my happiness, even my life fade away.

Mutt' Teille, Teille,

But, for you, for you

kansani ja maani,

my people and my country,

mä Teille huokaan
vielä kuollessain.

for you I shall sigh even at the moment of my death.

I had been in this job for several weeks now, and the matron was very pleased with my work but, after all, I had been trying my best. Sometimes the other girls pulled all kinds of small pranks, in which I was not involved, fortunately. Once the girls received quite a scolding from the matron for having stayed out much too late. Then she came to thank me for not running around with the others, and she told me to keep on staying away from such amusements. Of course she did not know that I was still only a child, not yet old enough to be interested in such entertainment.

Then I received a couple of interesting letters. The first letter was from my Father. He told me in his letter that he had met Hilda's mother who had given him quite a sermon because he had not waited for her arrival from Finland, but had married. But then she had boasted that she could have her choice of men, as they knew she had money. She was planning to build a good house, a home for her sons, and she was intending to make her daughter move to this country, too.

(To be continued)

Episode 20, 10 Sep 1954

The second letter came from Canada. I looked at it, amazed, before I opened it. Surely that handwriting had to belong to my foster sister Maria, and indeed the letter was from Maria. She wrote that in Sweden she had gotten engaged to a young man called Richard Laine, but that he had then crossed

118

the Atlantic and gone to Toronto. He had sent a ticket to Maria, and as soon as she had arrived in Toronto, they had gotten married. In her letter she was now deploring how hard it was to manage without knowing the language, and she asked me to come and help her, as she thought I must now be able to manage in English, having been here for so long.

I wrote back to my Father at once, promising for sure to come home in the spring. To Maria I wrote only a brief note, telling her that I now had a good job and I had not thought of leaving to yet another completely unknown land.

The "dining room girls" were nice Norwegians, from Iowa. They had left the farm to earn more money. The girl called Lisi loved horses a lot. Once she said to me: "Anni, why don't you come with me, let's go and rent a horse and a carriage from the livery barn for a couple of hours, so we can go and ride around." And that is what we did on one Sunday, when we both had the day off. Lisi was a good driver, and the two-wheeled carriage was comfortable. It was such a fun and memorable ride. We counted every church along our way, and the total was eleven. Well, the people in this town sure are religious, we were saying.

Every day, a local farm delivered milk and cream to this hotel, and it was one of my chores to receive the delivery and put it in the storage room. The milk was delivered by a tall, slender young man called Fred. He began to pay me attention, chatting about everyday things. Once, when he was delivering the milk, he also gave me a bouquet of beautiful white roses. I said thank you and took the roses to my room. Perhaps a week later he brought me roses again. Now they were yellow, and the next time they were pink. The girls began to tease me: "Now Anni has got a boyfriend, she will surely start going out at night." But I was just amused by this whole romance.

Once when the milkman was bringing me roses again, the girls were quick to steal them from his hands before he managed to give them to me. Fred thought of a way to avoid this. The next time he had put the roses in an empty milk can, and whispered to me: "The roses are in the milk can in the ante-room, you can go get them there." I went and got the roses and they were red "American Beauty" roses. The girls found it odd that I did not get any roses. They had not seen me take the roses to my room via the back stairs, and when they came into my room that night they could not help but wonder how the roses ended up in my room after all. I myself began to wonder what this abundance of roses could possibly mean, and all of a sudden I remembered the phrase, "Say it with flowers". It must have been Fred's way of courting me, and I did not need to wonder about it much longer, as an actual love letter arrived in the mail to me from Fred. It was written in a good hand, in English of course, and he said he was madly in love with me, and he was asking me to marry him though I had never even gone out with him, not even once. In any case, it was my very first real love letter. I took it to Lisi, and after she had read it she gave a long whistle and asked: "What are you going to answer, Anni?"

I just burst out laughing, and said: "Why what do you think I am going to answer, for I don't know this man at all, and secondly, I would not accept any man of any nationality other than my own, and thirdly,

I don't know enough English to write him an answer anyway." Lisi said: "Don't worry, just think what you want to say, I will write a model for you in pencil, so you can answer him." I did so, and that was the end of that love story.

I was wondering whether Tauno would write to me like that from South Dakota, or whether he would write at all. Toimi had written to me a couple of times from Finland, asking me to wait, saying he might also come to America one day. I also got letters from Antti, whom I had met a few days before Father and I left for his homestead. And Vilho, The neighboring homesteader's son, had written too, hoping I would come home soon, even for a quick visit.

An old man took over the milk deliveries. But the last roses had not withered yet when the matron came and whispered in my ear, that there was a "little Finn boy" waiting for me in the office, and I should go and see him. I blushed up to my ears and did not know what to do, and the matron told me to "go on, go on now".

In the office, there was the young man I had met soon after my arrival from Finland. He had been introduced to me by the wife of the young family with whom my Father had lived at the time. He greeted me and said he had written to me, but because he had not received any replies, he had decided to come and see me.

I did remember receiving a couple of letters from him, but I had written back. He said he had thought I might have written back, because once he had found a letter addressed to him, by the road, torn in pieces He was guessing that as my Father picked up everyone's mail at the station, he had recognized my handwriting, opened the letter and then thrown it away. (Later when I was visiting home, Father did tell me he had done so.)

Karl wanted to talk to me longer, but I said I had to go back to work, but if he wanted to, he could take a room in the hotel, and then that night I could speak with him.

That night we went for a walk in the park and just talked of things that had happened at home. He wanted to see me again on the following night, but I said it would be expensive for him to stay at the hotel, and boring, too, so he could just as well leave. But first I went and got one of Fred's roses, and I pinned it on Karlo's breast.

He left, and again the girls teased me an awful lot about the "little Finlander". I got letters from him, but I did not reply to any of them, and finally the letters stopped coming.

One morning I was in the kitchen, bent over the counter, peeling some vegetables. The master walked past and, why, he gave me a slap in passing. Oh if it did not scare me, and I asked: "Have I done something wrong?" He said: "Whom the God loves, he shall also punish," and went away, laughing.

The master and the matron were Catholic, but the matron went to the church alone early on Sunday mornings. The employees did not have to get up so early, so she went out without having so much as a cup of coffee. When I noticed it, I got dressed, rushed into the kitchen, made some good coffee and put it on a tray, along with some pastries. Then I went upstairs and knocked on her door. She opened the door and looked me in the eyes, questioningly, but when she saw the tray I was holding, and on it the steaming coffee, her eyes lit up and she said, "No one has ever been so kind to me. I was just on my way to the church. Thank you, dear child."

After that, I would take her coffee every Sunday morning. And she rewarded me. Often, at night, when I was the last person in the kitchen, prepping something, and she would come to lock the storage room, she would ask me to come into the storage room, then she would give me all kinds of fruit, and say I could take the fruit up to my room and eat them whenever I liked.

(To be continued)

Episode 21, 14 Sep 1954

I had not taken any leave time for several months, so one day I asked the matron if I could have a couple of days of leave. She looked at me slyly and asked why. I told her about my stay in the biggest town of Minnesota, how I had arrived from the countryside knowing nothing about anything, and how my good cousins had welcomed me, and helped me in every possible way with clothing, jobs and American manners. I had been saving my wages, and now I was ready to repay my cousins at least what they had spent on my behalf. The matron was happy for me to go, and when I arrived at my cousins', they were all as friendly as ever, however I no longer spoke Finnish as purely as before, because during the several months of my employment, I had not heard a single word of Finnish, except the day Karl came to visit me. Every now and then a "well" or a "but" or some other short English word popped up in my speech, and finally I said to my cousins: "Well, now I'm in a bad way, aren't I." Amazed, they asked me in unison,"What did I mean". I said: "I have forgotten Finnish, and I cannot speak English."

When I returned to work from my fun-filled and refreshing vacation, I was no longer happy, though everything was as it was before. Even the girls noticed my wistfulness, and they suggested that I go out with them that night. I joined them, as after all I had finished confirmation school before leaving the countryside to work in town. We went to the park to listen to some music. The girls had gotten acquainted with some young men. They introduced them to me, and one of them, Harry, seemed to seek my company more than the others. He always had a lot of funny stories to tell, but I was not all that keen on their company, so I left them, and on Sunday afternoons I would just go and sit down by the lake, by myself, singing:

Yksin istun ja lauleskelen,	I'm sitting here alone and singing
kun aikani on niin ikävä.	as I am feeling so melancholy.
Vesi seisoo ja linnut laulaa,	The water is still and the birds are singing,
eikä tuulikaan värähdä.	and there isn't the slightest breeze.

I was wondering to myself whether I was in love, but with whom? I didn't know, I was just homesick,

124

that's all. But I did sing a couple of songs:

Oi jos lempi luotu	Oh, were it that love
ei oisi ollenkaan	had never been created
Niin moni raukka rauhan	So many unhappy people
tuntisi rinnassaan.	could feel peace in their breast.

Well, nothing else would do; I decided to go home. I reckoned there would be good jobs available closer to home. I started making travel preparations. Now I had so much clothes that I had to buy a travel trunk. I resigned from my job, and the matron was ever so sorry, but when I told her I was very much homesick, she said: "You may come back whenever you want." So I got everything ready. First I had to go to St. Paul which was just a short distance away, and there I would catch a long-distance train home. All went well up to that point, but when I was going to buy that long-distance ticket at the railway station ticket booth, my money came up ten cents short. Oh, the things an inexperienced child does unthinking. I had put the rest of my money in the new travel trunk, keeping with me only what I thought the train ticket would cost, and now the trunk was in the baggage car. I said to the station manager that I had put my money in the trunk. And now the trunk was on its way somewhere. The station manager said angrily: "It's a wonder you didn't put your keys in the trunk as well." It seemed like a stupid thing to say, but then again,

125

what was I, if not stupid.   There I was now, sitting on a bench at the great railway station of St. Paul, and I suppose I was crying, when a kind looking old woman walked up to me. I looked up, with tears in my eyes, and saw that she was wearing a badge of some sort that said "Travelers Aid", or something like it. She asked: "Why are you so sad, young lady?" and, amidst my sobs, I explained my problem. She sat down next to me and said: "Now why don't you pour all your money in your lap and let me count it for you first." I did so, and there was a lot of small change. She counted it quickly and said: "Now let's count it again, together." We did, and she said: "Oh, but there is enough money, now let me go and buy that ticket for you with your money, and where was it again that you wanted to go?" We went to the ticket booth, and just then the station manager announced the departure of the northbound train. The woman pressed the ticket in my hand, and I thanked her and asked for her name and address. She had a card in her pocket that she gave me, and she took me to the steps of the train and wished me a good trip. I still don't know whether I was so nervous that I counted my money wrong, or whether that kind lady added a few pennies and I never noticed. At the first opportunity, I bought a pretty sofa cushion cover and mailed it to her, along with a brief letter.

At home I saw at once that many changes had taken place. It was no longer necessary to pick up the mail at the small railway station, but a carriage drawn by a pair of horses delivered it to mailboxes by the roadside, because now there was a road leading through the area. However it did not lead past my home, it went past the lands of my uncle who was

126

living on the opposite shore of the lake, and it was there that all the settlers had put their mailboxes, and they took turns picking up everyone's mail, just a mile away, when one took shortcuts through the woods. A small school had been built, and the teacher was living nearby.

As soon as I got home, the word of my arrival went around, and neighbors dropped in to say hello. Those days at home flew as if on wings. It was winter and weather was excellent for skiing. As I was circling the lake on skis, I remembered many a skiing competition from my school days. There was a small hotel in a nearby township. They needed a matron, and when the owner of the hotel came to ask me to work for them, he did not even ask how old I was. We agreed upon the date when he would come and pick me up. It happened to be the date of my Mothers death. Several years afterwards, something good would happen to me on that day, so I thought it was as if Mother was taking care of her little girl in spirit, after her death. While Mother was alive, it was Maria who had meant everything to her, however.

Of course I went, and it turned out to be a really nice job, because I had no one "bossing" me. As soon as the master took me into the kitchen, he told me that here I was in charge all by myself, because his wife had her own job in the store. I was so happy that I could do everything exactly as I wanted, and now I was free to put to use the cooking lessons I had learned from the cookbook, and from my work experience. I would not have traded it for any kind of school. This job was all the more practical because the master told me to just go get everything I needed in the store.

In this family there were two daughters. One of them went to school in the eastern states for some of the summer, and the other started in the autumn. Both girls were older than I was, and they intended to study "high". It is curious but I did not envy them at all. This household was a cosy place to live and work. If there were guests, they would be served first, and when the family came into the dining room after the guests, they never started eating before they called: "Anni, why don't you come and join us now." They always wanted me to join them at mealtimes, so in their home I never felt like a servant, but a member of the family. Sometimes, when the daughters happened to be in the kitchen when their father came in, he would catch all three of us and hold us in his arms and say: "Here is my three-leaved clover."

Once a roomful of Indians arrived, and when they sat down in the "ofiisi", their loud talking carried into the kitchen, and I was afraid and wondered to myself how to cook food and serve it to such a loud crowd.

Their boss came into the kitchen and said I did not need to be afraid though they were loud, just go ahead and fix them a lot of "everyday" food. He said he was taking them to a logging camp, but they had had to stop at this station to change trains, and as it happened to be mealtime, he had brought them here to eat.

(To be continued)

Episode 22, 17 Sep 1954

A small hotel like this one had to have plenty of

food in store at all times, because occasionally a lot of people might turn up without any advance warning whatsoever. That is how we were now able to serve the Indians a large meal. They kept talking to me when I brought in new dishes. I kept saying thank you politely, though I did not have the faintest idea of what they were prattling about, or if they were criticizing the food. Finally the last one left the table, and did I ever heave a sigh of relief. Then the boss came in to say that the Indians had been very pleased with the meal. But oh my goodness what the tables looked like after them: all sorts of food had dropped on the white table clothes, even on the floor.

I set the tables all over again for our regular patrons. They included two railway officials, and five men from the saw mill. They began to tease me that I should have such gentlefolk dining here every day.

I did my work with great care, but it did not prevent me from making all kinds of observations of my surroundings. In any outsider's eyes, the family seemed happy. The father and the oldest daughter were cheerful and good-natured. The mother and the youngest daughter were more serious and grumpy. I always noticed that the master often went out at night, always walking in the same direction. The first thing I noticed was that the master and the mistress never went out together, and they always spoke to each other with cold formality. Then the independence day (the Fourth of July) came, and a great dance was going to be held that night at the local entertainment hall. Both daughters were at home then, and it seemed that after the dinner the whole family was preparing to go to the dance. I did not dance, so I was waiting for the family to go out, looking forward to a nice evening alone in my room upstairs, reading a good book. As soon as I heard everyone leaving, I settled comfortably to read my book.

It was ever so sweet and quiet. The pleasant fragrance of the lilac trees floated in through an open window. I had been reading for a while and I set the book down to give my eyes a little rest, when I heard something from downstairs. It was a door, opening and closing quietly, but I was not worried, thinking it was just one of the family members. Whatever happened this late in the day did not concern me. I went back to my reading, but began to feel a bit restless. What if something happened downstairs after all and they would blame it on me. I tried to put it out of my mind and just go on reading.

I do not know how long I had been reading, when I heard something again. Someone was talking, but I could not make out the words. Then my curiosity got the better of me and I put down my book. Without making a sound I tiptoed to the hall and the top of the stairs, where I could see downstairs. A door opened quietly downstairs, and light fell from the room to the hall, where a beautiful, middle-aged woman was standing. I heard a man's voice whisper: "Good-bye my darling Ella, we'll meet again soon." The door through which the light had shone to the hall closed quietly, then so did the front door, and the woman was gone. Then everything was quiet. I crept back into my room, but though I picked up my book, I could not concentrate on reading, because I knew the woman who had left, and I knew the voice that had told her good-bye. Finally I went to bed, remembering that a new work day would begin for me in the morning, but I could not sleep. Then I heard the front door opening and closing, and the girls chattering happily about their night out, and soon everything was quiet again. I fell asleep and woke up to the sound of my alarm clock. At the breakfast table, the girls had plenty to tell, they had had such a good time, and their mother joined them. The master, however, did not say a word.

Life resumed its usual path, with some small exceptions. When I went to the town, I saw several times that beautiful woman whom I had just glimpsed at that night of the Forth of July, and I came to learn more about her. She was the wife of a local farmer, and a mother of five children, but she was from one of the Eastern states.

My boss, Mr. Ford was from the same town. As a young man he had been engaged to this beautiful woman, but then some major disagreement had occurred between them. Mr. Ford had married the girl next door then moved at once to this town in Minnesota. They built their home here, and after the great fire of Hinckley, Mr. Ford had amassed quite a large fortune. He had bought up a lot of land and forest, he had founded a saw mill, and he had built a large building with a store, where also the local post office was located later. Mrs. Ford became the private keeper of the store and the post office, while her husband's time was spent running various logging operations, and sawmill. In the meanwhile this beautiful Mrs. Steel had found out where Mr. Ford lived, and moved to the same town. Old love had rekindled into new flames. A couple of years later some changes took place, but I shall tell about them in due course.

Now I shall tell about a really nice family I met while working at the Fords. They lived just a couple of streets down from the Fords. This family consisted of the father, mother, four daughters and two sons. In the friendly company of this family I spent many nice evenings that summer. Sometimes, at their request, I would stay there quite late, and of course my employers thought that I was spending my nights with a boyfriend. They would tease me, but I did not explain where I had been. Once Mr. Ford said, if you, Anni, were to marry while you live here, I shall throw you a lavish wedding, and pay for everything. Having said this, he cast a crafty look at a particular young man at the table who had just much praised the doughnuts I had made. I just laughed, and said, "Well, I'm not in a hurry, Mr. Ford."

I have said earlier that in those days all Finns felt as if they were all related to each other. Thus, during my visits to the Finnish family, Mrs. Ikola took me as if under her wing, and gave me plenty of good advice for my life. Some of her advice, as I shall tell later, was not really all that "good", though her intentions were the very best. Often, at night, when the young members of the Ikola family began to retire for the night, Mrs. Ikola would say: "Anni, don't go just yet, let's you and I stay up a little longer and have a chat." Then she told me many things about her youth, and eventually also about her childhood sweetheart with whom she had made a firm agreement to marry, but on sudden impulse she had decided otherwise, and she had come here, to the golden land in the west, ending up a wife and mother here.

Now she had received a letter from a friend of hers, with the news that her former boyfriend had also come to this country and that after several inquiries he had found out where Mrs. Ikola lived. In the letter, the friend also said that that man was going to come and meet Mrs. Ikola as soon as possible. "Oh, dear Anni, what should I do now, suppose he is coming here to pay me back for my unfaithfulness", moaned Mrs. Ikola "I'm afraid this worrying is going to make me ill", she continued.

(To be continued)

Episode 23, 21 Sep 1954

Her story was making me nervous, too, but I tried to calm her down, saying: "Well, a sensible man can't possibly mean you any harm. Suppose he just wants to see you, just like that other man in this country. He wanted to see his former beloved in Finland, and the poem goes like this:

Jos kiikari ois',	If I had a pair of binoculars
jolla näkisi	with which I could see
yli Atlantin meren aavan,	across the wide open Atlantic Ocean,
niin vanhaan maahan	at my old country
sen suuntaisin,	I would point it,
että näkisin vielä sen Taavan	so I could see that Taava one more time.
Että onko sillä paljon lapsia?	Does she have

	many children
Ja muuttunut onko muoto?	And has her appearance changed?
Onko kasvot käyneet kurttuihin?	Has her face grown all wrinkled?
Onko köyryny selkäruoto?	Is her back now all bent?
Hän oli niin nätti nuorena;	She was so pretty when she was young,
hän oli kuin tuomen kukka.	like the blossom of the bird cherry tree.
Mutt' en ollut silloin minäkään	But back then, neither was I
tällainen . äijä rukka.	the hunched old man I am now.

Then Mrs. Ikola burst out laughing, and said: "Oh, Anni, you always find something funny to say at the right time and the right place, thank you for that. But, now tell me quite honestly, Anni, how is it with you and love affairs? Have any of your admirers seemed more pleasing than the others?"

"Well, no", I had to answer, "I have not fallen in love for real yet. But I have been waiting for one of my fellow travelers, Tauno, to write to me. I did tell you that Tauno went to Dakota and he promised to write, and we even agreed to meet again in the place where we last parted. But that was three years ago, he might well have forgotten me, as I was just a child back then." "Well, he is hardly the only pebble on the lake shore", said Mrs. Ikola. "But here's what I have been thinking: why don't you wait a little so I can be your mother-in-law. You must have noticed the admiring looks our Teuto keeps casting at you so often? He will grow up soon, though he is a bit younger than you are. And so I have an excellent proposal for you, along with some good advice.

Now, tell me first how many friends do you already have, all in all?" Mrs. Ikola finished her speech. I was somewhat amazed at her words, but I said, "They're just acquaintances. That's all. Well, first there is Toimi back in Finland, then my fellow traveler Tauno in Dakota; Antti, whom I met when I came to America, the boy who came to see me all the way beyond St. Paul; and then my Father's neighbor's son Vilho whom I cannot forget; and in that English-speaking town I met Harry." "Well, how about Peter?" asked Mrs. Ikola.

"Didn't your boss, Mr. Ford already promise to organize a wedding for him and you?" she continued. "You can forget all about it, and that goes to any other business of that kind", I replied curtly.

"Well, then, Anni, stop all your letter writing and dating for a while, and then the boy who finds his way back into friendship with you, he will be the right one! Do you understand, Anni?" she asked. "Yes, I do, Mrs. Ikola", I answered. "But please don't forget all about our Teuto, dear Anni?" "No, I won't", I replied, though my thoughts were already a-wondering entirely elsewhere.

I got a week's leave from work, and I decided to go home to see my family. Master said that Anni should be driven home by horse and carriage, and so the young man working there brought the horses and a light carriage in front of the house. I was just about to get in the carriage, when Master came out of the house and told us to wait. Then Master walked to the carriage and said to John: "Hand me the reins, I shall take Anni home myself." John looked at him in amazement, and his cheeks flushed with anger as he hesitantly stepped down. Master Ford stepped into the carriage and started driving fast down the good road. I was afraid, though I did not rightly know why. I wanted to ask him something, but I did not dare.

Finally Master Ford broke the silence, starting to talk of this and that everyday thing. Then he began to say something about his wife, but I had anticipated what he was going to say, and so I tried in every possible way to change the subject. I said that Mrs. Ford is such a hard-working lady, and pretty, too. In response, Mr. Ford grumbled something indistinct.

Now the road was beginning to get worse. This road had used to be just a foot path, but nowadays, in dry weather, horses could take it, too. However, lately there had been heavy rains, and further away the road seemed even worse. The carriage began to sink in the mud up to its axle, and I was very much afraid, but Mr. Ford was just laughing, until the road got absolutely hopeless, and he said he had to turn around. He had to unharness the horses and tie them up to a tree. Then he lifted me from the carriage and set me down in a dry spot. He began to work the carriage out of the mud, one wheel at a time, managing finally to turn it, as it was just a light carriage. He said he was sorry he could not take me all the way home, and that he hoped that having to walk the remaining distance would not make me tired. I thanked him and said it would be just a nice, short walk, and I sighed in relief when I saw Mr. Ford driving away fast, so I did not have to listen to his story. I heard it years later, but not from Mr. Ford.

Soon I regained my usual good mood, and walked happily towards my home, singing:

Lempeitä laakson lehtoja	Those gentle glades in the valley
ja lintujen laulupuistoja	and the lands where the birds would sing
ja marjaisia kankaitaan	and the fields where berries grew
en unhoittaa voi milloinkaan.	I cannot ever forget.

I could not have imagined the surprise that was waiting for me at home. Father greeted me at the door, and when I stepped inside, walking towards me from the other end of the room, hand extended, was Uncle Lönroos.

Oh, but it was the warmest of greetings. He said that I had grown and changed so much that he could not have recognized me for the five-year girl who said good-bye to him at the Helsinki harbor, but then again, it had happened eleven years ago.

Uncle said I had grown up to look a lot like Aunt Linda. I found it very flattering, because Aunt was such a beautiful woman, and at home back in Finland, only Maria had ever been called beautiful. Uncle had so much to talk about. He asked about what Aunt Linda had talked about, had she ever talked about the past, was Aunt Linda happy, and so on. He had very little to say about himself. He said he had been very homesick when he came to America. He had bought some land, complete with buildings. He had lived there for a while, but he had just been thinking of Aunt Linda all the time, regretting that he had let go of her so easily. Then he had met a downhearted widow, and taken her as his companion in life, only because living alone had been unbearable, and also because in that way he could help the widow who had been left with a young son to survive the batterings of this world.

(To be continued)

Episode 24, 24 Sep 1954

I listened to Uncle Lönroos' story, thinking that life truly does lead us down some very strange roads, and in my mind came a song that maybe described Uncle's feelings:

Lemmen liekki kans'	Often the flame of love
useast' sammuup'	may also go out
Rakkaus kauniskin	Even the most beautiful love
katoo pois.	may fade away
Syömmen sisuspuol'	Then the inside of one's heart
silloin tummuup	grows dark.
Ah kemp' ei Oh,	but who would not drink
rintansa riemuks' jois.	to try and cheer

138

Liukas on maailman tie.   up their heart.
                                           Slippery are the
                                           roads of this
                                           world.

My week of leave passed quickly, and I said good-bye to Uncle Lönroos and wished him all the best. He said he too would go home soon, as he was expecting his brother's son, Kustaa, to arrive from Finland. He was going to leave everything to Kustaa who had been working for the Finnish railways, but was hoping to find something better in America.

Back at work, I was happy to find nothing "extra" waiting for me. The girls had been good housekeepers, but they were happy to leave it all to me again. The railway officials were fretting that in my absence they had not had any tasty Finnish coffee bread, so I promised to bake some the very first thing.

Even on my leave, I had been thinking a lot about Mrs. Ikola's story, trying to imagine what Mrs. Ikola's "first love" was like, and whether he had really traveled to see his former "sweetheart". The Ikolas had always received me as such a welcome visitor that I decided to go and see them the very following night.

The girls ran to meet me when they saw me coming, and almost in unison they said, "He is here now". But he was entirely different from what their mother had feared and expected. He had not spoken a single word of the past, but had come to the house as if an old family friend. He had toured the farm and other sights with Mr. Ikola, and when we girls went in, Mr. Ikola and "He" was already there, seated at the coffee table, having what seemed a good conversation. I was introduced to "Him" as a friend of the girls. Mrs. Ikola looked at me, her expression still full of uncertainty, but I gave her a look which I hoped she would read as saying "didn't I say so".

Now the days were going by somewhat monotonously. I began to feel like I could not stand it for much longer, and I decided that in a month's time I would go to the town where I had first arrived from Finland, to join my Father. I had already heard of a good job there. One night, I was sitting in my room, reading a poetry book sent to me by a female relative in Finland. I was thinking of my fellow traveler, Tauno, in Dakota, surely he had forgotten me ages ago. I read a poem in the book:

Sua unhoittaa pois	To forget you
en mä vois,	I cannot,
vaikk' kuolo mulle	even if remembering you
sen muiston tois.	brings me my death.
Sua hetken vain,	For a moment only
mä nähdä sain.	did I gaze at you.
Mutt' kuvas ei katoo	But the vision of you
mun muistoistain.	will not vanish from my mind.
Se on vain hetken työ,	It takes but a moment
kun salama lyö,	for the lightning to strike

mutt' ikuisen jäljen	yet a permanent mark
se puuhun syö.	it carves in the wood.

Oh, it was easy for Mrs. Ikola to instruct me to forget all my acquaintances, but quite another thing for me to do so. Despite everything, I sank into my daydreams. In my mind's eye, I saw that strong and willowy Finnish athlete boy, Tauno, jump from the train to the platform, even before the train comes fully to a halt, then he will catch me, a mere slip of a girl, in a passionate embrace. But, had I known how our reunion would turn out a couple of weeks later, my beautiful dreams would have received quite a blow. That is why it is a good thing that we have no advance knowledge of our lives.

I shall describe my reunion with Tauno a bit later. For the time being, I was just living in rosy daydreams.

The next time I went to see the Ikola family they were talking about the visitor who had come and gone. Mrs. Ikola went about her chores as if asleep, and very absent-minded. I began to tease her a little, saying: "Your life has been just like in that old song:

Vanno siis, Hulda,	So, swear to me, Hulda,
täss' taivahan nähden	as Heaven stands witness,
ett' voin sinuun luottaa	that I can trust you
jos minne mä lähden.	no matter where I shall go.

To that, you would reply:

Yksin vain Hjalmarin morsian	Only Hjalmar's fiancée
mä oon.	shall I be.
Jos muiden,	Should I go with others,
niin taivas mun rangaiskoon.	may Heaven punish me.

And so, for all those years, you were afraid of a punishment from above, but your greatest punishment turned out to be just a bad conscience, didn't it?"
"Well, I am rid of it now," said Mrs. Ikola.

I would have had some news to tell to Mrs. Ikola, but I hesitated, because of her recent advice to stop all my correspondence. Now I had gotten a letter from Tauno, to my great astonishment. He was asking if I still remembered how we had decided to meet again, and where we had decided to meet. Why, where we had parted, and how could I possibly not remember! Hardly a day had gone by that I had not been thinking about it, which was why I had decided to go and find a job in that town, hoping to meet Tauno. I wrote back at once, saying I would be in town when he arrived, at the end of the harvesting season.

Mrs. Ikola noticed my silence, and asked, "What are you thinking about, Anni?" Before I replied, the older Ikola girls began again to talk about the visitor. One of them said that she would have liked to have him as their father, but the older girl snapped angrily: "What nonsense, I for one think our own father is the

142

best in the world!" Mrs. Ikola was listening to them, looking so helpless, that to me it seemed absolutely ridiculous.

Both girls of the Ford family were again at home for a while. Several young people dropped by every night. I noticed that one of the railway officials boarding at the Fords' was seeking the younger girl's company, while the older girl had the tall and handsome Irish boy for company. There was also Peter to keep me company. When we were sitting on the porch, he talked of how "we" might perhaps make a home for us, and more in a similar vein. Then he suggested that we go out on the following Saturday night, and I promised to go. But then, one night that week, we girls were in the kitchen, and of course the talk soon turned to boys. The girls were talking about their plans for the coming Saturday, and I exclaimed, "there is not a single boy in this village with whom I would go out". After that, we laughed and had a good time.

Soon the awaited Saturday night arrived. I dressed up with great care, and waited in my room, looking at the clock every now and then. One hour after another went by, and I began to cry in annoyance and anger. Finally I went to bed.

(To be continued)

Episode 25, 28 Sep 1954

The next day, when I saw Peter, I pretended not to notice him at all, and for several days I managed to avoid giving him an opportunity to speak to me. Then,

143

one night, I was sitting by myself on the porch, in the twilight. By then I had overcome my hurt feelings and felt I could make fun of any boy whomsoever. I saw Peter walking towards me, but before he could say a word, I said: "Well if it isn't the boy who jilted me and broke my heart in tiny pieces; are you happy now?" I said a lot of other things, too, and even laughed at him mockingly. Then Peter took my hand firmly in his and said: "Anni, listen to me, isn't it my turn to speak now? Do you remember one night last week when you and the girls were in the kitchen, having such a laugh? And you said that there was not a single boy in this village with whom you would go out, although you had already promised to go out with me. At that moment, I was just about to come into the kitchen, and I could not help overhearing your words. I turned around at the doorstep and left, and that is why I did not come to pick you up. Anni, I am an honest man, do you think I have no honor? You better go at once and tell the girls that you did not mean what you said that night."

"And that's something I shall never do; our parting is just a 'happy accident'," I said, and ran into my room, leaving Peter to stare after me in amazement.

After that, I received two more proposals of marriage. One of them was from a man well past his middle age. He was wealthy, and of course he reckoned that a young slip of an emigrant girl would be happy to accept such an offer. He promised me a good life, saying: "It is better to be an old man's beloved than a young man's slave." I said no to both proposals, without asking for any time for consideration.

Naturally, I believed I was the master of my fate, and I was thinking of the fate of Mr. Ford which the following verses seemed to describe fittingly:

Oi jos lempeä luotu	Oh, were it that love
ei olis ollenkaan,	had never been created
Niin moni raukka tuntis	So many unhappy people
rauhan rinnassaan.	could feel peace in their breast.

But who knows of the events in their lives ahead of time, or would even like to know. The younger daughter began to prepare her wardrobe for her upcoming trip to the Eastern states. When she noticed that I stayed at home at nights, in my room, with a book or some piece of handicraft, she asked me to help her with her preparations. She gave me the task of hand sewing fine hem decoration on her dress. I wondered whether it was part of my duties to spend my own free time on such household chores. I sewed very little, and very carelessly. That trick worked. She said I could go, and she did not ask for my help in evenings again. And I thought it was better to start going out again at night.

Once, when I went to see the Ikola family, Mrs. Ikola came to meet me at the door, exclaiming happily: "Oh, it is so good that you came, Anni, because the girls and I have been wondering whether you're cross with us for some reason." I said: "Of course I am not, there is no reason whatsoever, and I shall always remember the kindness this whole family has shown to me." "But why would you say something like that, Anni, are you going to leave somewhere?" asked Mrs. Ikola. . "Well, I have mentioned to you that I might go to the town, and now I have decided to go, so actually I came to say good-bye to you, my dear friends, and thank you a thousand times for all your kindness and advice. I will come and visit you again one day." I was already standing by the door, when Mrs. Ikola realized that Teuto was not there, and she began to call: "Hallo, Teuto! Aren't you going to come and say good-bye to Anni?" Teuto arrived, blushing, and I said to him: "Good-bye, my young friend. We'll meet again one day."

In town, I found a job equal to the one I had had before, but I was having a hard time feeling at home in this household, even though the mistress was friendly. There were grown-up daughters in this family, too, but I did not feel like a member of the family. There was a black girl working with me, she came in for the days and lived elsewhere. From the very beginning, she made a very bad impression on me. I noticed that she had a tendency to do all kinds of filching. Often the mistress let me know when something had gone missing again.

The storage cupboard of the house was placed on the porch where it could be seen from the kitchen. Once again, fruit and pastries had disappeared from the cupboard, and the mistress told me about it. It made my honest Finnish blood boil, and I said to her: "I always eat very reasonable meals, and I never need to steal any extra snacks." The following afternoon the mistress happened to be in the kitchen just as I was making bread dough. She happened to

146

look out on the porch, and there was the black girl gobbling up delicacies at that very moment.

When the girl came back into the kitchen, I said to the mistress: "Now I have been watching this for long enough and I have come to the conclusion that one of us kitchen maids must go. Either I go, or she goes, but I won't work with her any longer."

After that, the black girl did not come to work any more, and I was fully in charge of the kitchen duties. The mistress told me that she was going away for a couple of weeks, and she was going to ask her daughters to help me where necessary, because she had done most of the baking herself. Then the mistress left, and soon after that one of the girls fell sick. I said I had experience of baking and so I could do the baking now, but oh my goodness how badly my bread turned out. I was horrified but the girls just told me to try again, perhaps I would have better success the second time. But no, to my great annoyance the result was the same. I was afraid that the family would think I had been telling lies and that in fact I had never done any baking before. I tried to tell them that there was something wrong with the yeast, but did they believe it, and I was not all that certain of it myself. However, I decided to go to a different store, instead of the one that delivered to the house. I did not tell the girls about my plan. When I got the yeast, I began one more batch, alternating between fear and hope. Luckily the girls did not come into the kitchen until I was taking big, beautiful loaves out of the oven. These, just the kind of bread one can expect to make with the best flour. The girls were amazed. They said that not even their mother had baked such wonderful bread, and they wanted to know the secret behind this success. I told them I had gotten new yeast from a different store. Then one of the girls said that actually we ran out of yeast after mother left, but she found a chunk of old yeast on the cupboard shelf. She brought the old yeast to me thinking it was still good. But privately, I could not help thinking she had done it on purpose, to harass the poor little kitchen maid.

I worked here so dutifully that I didn't even go out much, even though I knew the addresses of several acquaintances. I was waiting for the mistress to come home and then I would have more time to go visiting. I had been in this job for several weeks now. The mistress had returned from her trip, and of course the girls told her everything that had happened, good and bad. She was ever so kind to me. She even brought me a present from Milwaukee just as she had for her own daughters. I tried to remember the addresses of the people I had visited with my Father when I first had arrived from Finland, but I could not be certain, as it had happened three years before.

(To be continued)

Episode 26, 1 Oct 1954

Servant folk usually had Thursday afternoon off. I was free so I decided to take a walk and see if I could find any familiar houses. Sure enough, I found none. I was just about to turn and walk back, when I saw a young policeman standing at the street corner. I went to him, apologized, and asked whether he could tell me how and where to find the street and

148

house I was looking for. He said: "Yes, of course," and he asked me several questions, such as when I had arrived in town, and was I planning to stay. Then he said he would walk with me, and take me all the way to the front door of the house I wanted to visit. I could hardly refuse his kind offer of help, but I kept wondering to myself, whatever were the passers-by thinking, seeing a young girl walking alongside a policeman. He was even so polite as to take my arm as we crossed the street. For reassurance, I kept reminding myself that at least he was chatting nicely with me, and we were laughing, so surely no one could think that this policeman was talking to some woman he had caught, and was now joking with her. I remembered the walks my Father and I used to take down these streets. Once there was a couple walking behind us, speaking Finnish so loudly that I could not help overhearing one of them say: "My, oh my, such a young girl has gone and married such an old man," and the other replied: "It is a pity, isn't it?" My Father heard them, too, and we were ever so amused, but we just kept walking on, hand in hand.

Thus, escorted by the policeman I made it to my destination, all the way to the front door, and I thanked him for his kindness, and went in. They were amazed I had found my way there. I did not bother to explain that I had a police escort. I just laughed that this town was nowhere near the size of London, and even there it was possible to get around without getting lost. It was a Finnish boarding house. The matron, Mrs. Salo, introduced to me several of the young men in the room, and conversation flowed easily, in the typical Finnish fashion. The afternoon was over so quickly, and soon I had to be going. One of the young men said that he would walk me back home. I was a little against it, but the matron said: "Well, my goodness, how can you turn down an escort."

We left, and so began a pleasant acquaintance. We found things to talk about all the way to the front door of the house where I worked. Then the young man asked whether he could come on Saturday night and take me to a show, and I promised to go. We did go out on several Saturday nights, to a show, or some other such entertainment. Later, I often wondered how we had so many things to talk about, even though we never discussed any personal matters. Politics, societal issues, and civilized entertainment, we covered them all as far as we understood them. I was happy to have found someone so serious and educated for company. If we went to see a show, we would most certainly form serious conclusions on what was acceptable or unseemly. This serious boy, Niilo, was a good conversation partner, not a topic was left untouched, from politics to the current situation in Finland. He kept abreast of the times by reading newspapers; he subscribed to several of them.

The matron of the boarding house had insisted that I visit again, on my Thursday afternoons off, so she could chat with me of all things Finnish. That is why I went there on one beautiful Thursday, wearing a new hat. The matron and I were having such a good conversation that we never looked outside. It had begun to rain, and the matron exclaimed: "Oh Anni, how are you going to get back home now, your pretty hat will get soaking wet."

A couple of young men who had been on the
night shift were having coffee with us. One of them

said he had a large umbrella and he would walk me back so my hat would not get wet. I thanked him for his politeness, and we left, but when we got to my door, he asked whether he could come and take me out on Saturday night. Absentmindedly, I said: "I suppose so." He said he would arrive at half past eight, if that was okay by me. I said again, I suppose so. He said goodnight and left.

I went into my room and then I remembered that Niilo had said that on Saturday night there was a good film on and he would pick me up at eight o'clock. Oh dear, I thought to myself, why on earth did I promise to this umbrella-carrying escort that I would go out with him. But then I consoled myself thinking that most likely he would not even remember asking me out, perhaps he had asked me just out of politeness, and so I forgot the whole matter. The film I saw on Saturday night with Niilo was indeed beautiful. In those days the films were just "silent pictures", but this film was in color, showing beautiful views from Colorado, and a phonograph was accompanying the film, playing the song "Silver Colorado".

When I got back, one of the girls said: "As soon as you left, a very handsome young man came here, he spoke such good English, and he was asking for you, Anni." All I could say was just: "Oh!" and I ran into my room.

When I next saw Niilo, he said that the handsome young man who had escorted me with his umbrella had told him that he had a "big date" that Saturday night with Anni; but Niilo had just thought he was teasing him, and come to take me out as agreed. He said that now Kusti would be singing:

Syksy vei, syksy vei	Autumn took away, autumn took away from me
minulta pois	
kukkaisen kukoistavaisen.	a blossoming flower.

A couple of weeks later I met a woman we both knew, and did she ever give me a thorough scolding. She did not even let me get a word in edgewise, to defend myself, when I tried to tell her that I had met Kusti just that once and could hardly call him my "boyfriend". She just kept on lecturing: "How did you, Anni, dare to turn down such a handsome boy," and: "He is well read, wealthy, he speaks good English, and he has a good job; where do you think you are going to find a better man, Anni?" I just blushed, and could not stammer a single word in my defense. Then I got a week's leave and went home. As usual, I had to get off at that small railway station from where I had first walked to my Father's homestead. A Finnish family was living there, and it was always nice to stop and visit with them for a while before going on that long road in the wilderness, but lately I had not had to walk any more, as Father had come to pick me up by horse and carriage. But this time, when Father had been here at the station and in this house, he had said to the mistress that he could not come and pick me up on the day I had mentioned in my letter, but he would come on the next day, or the day after that. That was why the daughters of the family had come to meet my train, and happily they told me that I would be staying with them for a day or two. Chatting and laughing, we arrived at the Niemelä house, and the mistress came happily to greet me, saying: "Well if it wasn't a happy accident that your father could not come and pick you up, so we get to keep you here, and we got a cook, didn't we? I can go about many outdoors chores, and you will cook," she said. I said I would be happy to. The master came in, too, and greeted me with: "Now it is just like we got us a daughter-in-law." "If only that were true one day," said Aino, the oldest daughter, teasingly. I asked: "Where is Vilho?"

(To be continued)

Episode 27, 5 Oct 1954

He was the family's eldest son, and we had been writing to each other, and I had always felt that in my heart there was a small tender spot reserved just for Vilho. It had been there since the very first day when he had happened to be at the railway station as I had first arrived, and as an aside my Father said then: "There's a decent lad, he is the oldest Niemelä boy."

That night, when all the day's work was done at the Niemelä's and we were sitting there, talking of this and that and the other thing, the mistress asked: "Anni, are you going to spend the winter in the town?" And when I said I had not decided yet, she said that it would be best for me to come and spend the winter here, in the countryside. Large logging operations were to start here soon, and they were going to build a bunkhouse where they would need a cook. "Reckon I'll get bored here," I said. "That's nonsense," said the mistress, "Vilho will come and see you in the evenings, and the girls too, and you can come and spend Christmas with us. Then you would be exactly as master Niemelä said yesterday, 'we would have a daughter-in-law' in the house. Vilho will come home for the winter, too, Anni, but you probably know that already." "I did meet Vilho once in the town," I replied, blushing.

When I went back to my workplace from my leave, the daughter of the family brought me a letter, saying: "It arrived while you were away." I said thank you and went to read it in my room. Even before I opened it, I guessed what it was about. It was from Tauno in Dakota, and he said he was coming to see me. I could not figure out my feelings at all. I was delighted, but also anxious, wondering to myself how the golden land of the west had affected the handsome Finnish athlete boy. I also wondered what Tauno might think of me. He would only remember a little girl, happy and brave, always ready to sing those beautiful Finnish songs that had resounded as we left our home country far behind us. Now I was almost grown up.

At last that long awaited night came. I dressed with great care; I could not wait for the moment of our meeting, but found myself sitting on the park bench much ahead of time. It took a great deal of willpower not to keep looking around. I just sat there, with a magazine, pretending to read it while attempting hard to stay calm and collected. Now I heard footsteps on the sandy path but I did not dare to look up just yet. The footsteps came closer. I stood up. Walking towards me was a man, old-looking, carelessly dressed, stumbling a little. My God! No, it

155

cannot be Tauno, it's some drunken layabout. I was going to walk away quickly, without looking at him, but he stepped in front of me, exclaiming: "Little Anni, is that really you?" He took my hand and said: "For sure, in three years a child has grown up, you have changed. You have become a pretty young lady. Will you come with me?" I actually stepped back, away from him. I could not stand his nearness and that stench of alcohol. I pulled my hand away from his. My mind was fairly flooded with words, but I was so stunned that I could not speak. Finally I managed to say: "Is this the change that the golden land in the west has wrought in you? Where is that upright athlete's posture? Oh Tauno, what would Mother Finland say now? Would she award you with medals and trophies?"

"Don't you start moralizing, Anni, just come with me, I've got at least three dollars left in my pocket," he said, pulling a couple of dirty and crumpled notes out of his pocket.

I could not help exclaiming: "Oh, Tauno, you! How differently did I imagine meeting you! I always remembered you as a handsome athletic young man, whom in my thoughts I learned to love, and I was feverishly looking forward to our reunion. But now I see that you have become a miserable victim of alcohol, whom I don't know any more, and what more, whom I don't even want to know." He put his hand in his pocket, jingled some money and said: "Anni, why do you talk like that. Come on, I've still got three dollars in my pocket. Let's go and get a license and get married." I said "I never wanted to marry a slave to alcohol, so this is good-by forever, but write to me sometime so I know how you are doing." He

156

extended his hand and said: "Goodbye Anni. You were too young and too good for me, but still I will never look for another, whether good, bad, young or old. And I will never write to you again."

I turned around and hurried away, almost running, without looking back. I felt as if I had woken from a nightmare, a dream that was never real, just imagination, the sort of love one feels when one reads a story and finds the hero of one's dreams there.

I could not stop wondering whether it was this country that destroyed brisk and sober young Finnish men. But one could hardly blame it on freedom, perhaps one could blame it on bad company, like in that saying about how one cannot help seeking like-minded company. Perhaps Tauno just lacked willpower so he was not strong enough to avoid or to want to avoid the kind of company that had turned him into a miserable wretch. I wondered what the members of the Tampere track and field club would have said if they had seen Tauno wobbling on the street, his hat foolishly tilted, wearing a bad suit: the club that only three short years earlier had awarded him so many medals for his outstanding performances in various sports disciplines. I also could not help remembering his words about us getting a marriage license. We had never even been together, except such a long time ago and when we had been nothing but traveling companions. A few letters could not have made us closer, and in any case, he ought to have remembered that I was not even of age yet. It was just nonsense cooked up by an alcohol-addled brain. I would not waste more of my time thinking about it any longer, I decided. Yet, had I died the day before, my thoughts would have forever remained pretty, rose-colored dreams. Today they had burst so suddenly, like pretty soap bubbles.

Almost running, I returned to my place of work. I slipped quickly into my room, threw myself onto my bed, and burst into uncontrollable tears. I was not crying out of disappointment, but out of grief, thinking how many decent young Finnish men would go astray here, ending up a slave to alcohol.

Several years after this incident, we read in the paper that Tauno had committed some gross deed, and afterward taken his own life in a small village in a neighboring state. He died a lonely man without any relatives in this country.

I remembered a couple of verses from a song that fit Tauno:

Kun minä tulin hurjaksi	When I turned wild
muuttui mun aikani kurjaksi	my days became misery
Mä mielin vain viinaa kavalaa	all I yearned for was deceitful booze

Again, I was going about my daily chores quite automatically, but at night, when the day's work was done, I would sit in my room and do some embroidery. I recalled my last visit at home, and the things my Father had told me.

He told me that Hilda's mother had turned her plans into reality. She had had a nice house built for her, complete with a sauna building. Then she had gone and taken some quiet, decent bachelor as her husband. Then she had bossed him and her twin sons around with no letup, so one of the boys had gone insane, and the other, in anger, had gone west. Even the husband had fallen so deep under Hilda's mother's command that he could not live in the house, but had to move into the sauna building. Then she had written to Hilda, telling her to come here, to her mother, even though Hilda was married and had a young son. The mother just ordered Hilda to leave her husband and son in Finland. Hilda had been against it, saying she was not even well enough to travel, but according to the latest news my Father had heard, Hilda was already on her way here, alone. That made me reminisce my childhood, and I hoped to meet Hilda again.

I was thinking a lot about mistress Niemelä's idea that I should leave the town for the winter, but I had not come to an agreement about it with myself just yet. Then, Thursday afternoon, I went to see an acquaintance of mine who was a matron at a boarding house, and I told her that now I had an opportunity to go away from the town, and spend the winter cooking for lumberjacks. When she heard where I was going to go, she got very excited, and said that it was not at all far from the place where her husband had filed a homestead, and they would go and settle there in the spring. They had no children, but they were hoping to start a real family life once they were settled in the countryside.

At this point, ahead of time, I cannot help telling about the life of this nice Finnish lady, although everything happened several years later. They did move to their homestead. They built a nice house, and they turned woodland into fields. When offspring was expected, she came into town while pregnant. Then she went back with a beautiful baby girl. This happened again two years later, and they had another daughter.

(To be continued)

Episode 28, 8 Oct 1954

But when they were expecting their third child, the baby, their third daughter, was born too early, at home, and the mother closed her eyes to this world for all eternity. It was such a heart-breaking incident. I was there when the baby of this hopeful pioneer mother was christened and fostered with an English-speaking family, and the mother was laid to rest in her grave. The two older girls were fostered with another English-speaking family. Their father vanished from the region completely. Their home was left to stand empty and rot away, but some remains are still there.

The girls grew up decent people, but not Finnish, even though both their mother and father had been full-blooded Finns. At school, other children had said to the younger girl: "The people you are living with are not your mum and dad, you are a Finlander." This poor foster mother still gets tears in her eyes when she remembers the day when her beloved little daughter ran home from school, crying, out of breath, saying "At school, the others said that I am not your daughter!" Many tears had to be shed before the matter was fully cleared. It makes one think, would it not be wiser to tell a child their true origin while they are still young.

Now I must leave those memories and return to

the moment when I was talking to the matron of the boarding house. I said to her: "In case I don't happen to visit before I leave town, if I leave, I shall wish you a good winter, and perhaps in spring we shall meet at your homestead. And thank you so much for all your wonderful company." "Thank you, dear Anni, for having come to cheer me up, because, as you know, I have always been too "busy" to go anywhere, and so I have been looking forward to each Thursday and your visit. All the very best to you, Anni," she said.

I was just about to leave, when Sulo, Niilo's brother, called from the other end of the room: "Wait for me, Anni, I'll come and walk you." "Don't bother, Sulo, no need to change brothers," I said, laughing, and left quickly.

I thought about Sulo a great deal on my way back. He was such a straight-backed, tall and blond-haired boy, the complete opposite of his brother. I could not help comparing the two of them. I was wondering what it would be like to spend time with him. I thought I had seen admiration in his eyes. But doubtless it had turned to anger when he heard my impolite reply. Well, no matter, I shall soon forget those brothers completely, I thought to myself.

The next Sunday night when Niilo came to take me out, we decided that we would go to the local library and borrow an American history book each and read it on weeknights, seeing as how we were both citizens. He had just received his second set of papers and I was naturalized on account of the naturalization of my father. Back in Finland, history had been just about the dreariest of all school subjects, religious history in particular, what with all those names and dates. Yet the history of this country seemed to capture our minds from the beginning. It might have also been because now our interest in learning was voluntary, while at school one was forced to study, whether one liked it or not.

One night we decided to go see a historical play. The tickets cost one dollar apiece, but we thought the play would be worth it, for we had just finished studying about this particular historical subject. Near the theater we met a neighbor of mine, a young man, and we suggested that he come and see the play with us. He did, but when the play was over and we left the building, he said that he would never ever again waste good money on something so useless. Yet we found the play well worth the admission fee.

Then it was the last Saturday night of my time in the town, as I was going to leave on the following Tuesday. Niilo came to take me to a song concert. They were performing such familiar and beautiful Finnish songs that one could not help wanting to join in on the singing:

Mustalaiseks' olen syntynyt,	I was born a gypsy
koditonna kuljeskelen nyt.	Now I roam about, homeless
Luonnon lapsi, mitä huolinkaan	Child of nature, what do I care
kun vaan vapahana olla saan.	as long as I can live free.

And there was another gypsy song, just as beautiful:

Tuli pohjasta äitini kulta,	My dear mother came from the north
isän Unkarin tuuli kai toi.	My father must have been carried by the winds from Hungary
Näin syntyissäin' nuotiotulta	When I was born, I saw the campfires,
ilolaulut ja viulut ne soi.	merry songs and fiddles were resounding.

During the intermission, we sat, chatting, and I was about to say that I was leaving town soon. I realized that the matron of the boarding house had not told Niilo about my visit last Thursday, thus I would have to tell Niilo myself tonight, but I decided to leave it until the very end of the evening.

The singing resumed, and I remembered how back in Finland my Father had always loved to listen to this song (he himself did not have a singing voice):

Kas Suomenlahdella hyrskyt	The surging waves of the Gulf of Finland
ja laajat Laatokan veet,	and the wide waters of the Lake Ladoga
ja vuolaat Tornion tyrskyt	and the swelling flow of the River Tornio

163

ja Maanselän harjanteet	the ridges of Maanselkä
Ne halkoo Suomea suurta	They split up the great Finland
ja pilkkoo kansaa sen.	and divide her people
Ne katkovat sammon juurta,	They break up the roots of the sampo
ei juurru se uudelleen.	and it cannot put down roots again.

Then they were singing this song:

On mulle Suomi suloisin	Finland is the country I love the most,
vaan Häme siitä kallehin.	and Häme is the most precious place there
Sen tuskin tiedän vertaista,	I know of no other place it's equal
niin kaunista, niin herttaista,	so beautiful, so sweet
kuin kulta Hämeen maa.	as is the beloved land of Häme

It made reminisce of my kind grandfather, there in Häme. Of course he is still living, I thought. I must write to him, and I must do it tonight. Then we heard this upbeat song:

| Honkain keskellä | Amidst pines |
| mökkini seisoo | my cabin stands |

and so on, and also this one:

| Suomi armas synnyinmaamme | Finland, land of |
| | our birth |

I became so homesick for Finland. Here I was, a poor little emigrant girl, struggling for my living in a foreign land. I remembered the day when I had first left for my job in the biggest town of Minnesota. Just as I was leaving my cousin's little boy came to me and he looked at me, with his head tilted, and said: "Poor little Anni, you must go away to earn your living".

Niilo gave me a gentle shove in the side and said: "What an earth are you daydreaming about, Anni. The concert is over, we must get going." "Going? Yes, going. I am going away next Tuesday," I managed to say. I had received a letter from a friend inviting me to spend autumn in the countryside. I was delighted and told Niilo of my decision. "Are you joking, Anni?" he said. "No, I am not. This is good-bye," I said. "Oh no, you cannot leave without me coming to see you on your last night here, or our love would be very cold indeed," he said. I burst into peals of laughter, and Niilo looked at me in amazement. Then I, too, turned serious and said: "What on earth are you doing, talking about love at the last moment? You never spouted such nonsense before. I have enjoyed your company so much, and we have always talked about all kinds of things, Finland's fate, current events, all kinds of pastime, but we never spoke about love. And now I would thank you for such good company, and I hope you have enjoyed my company this summer, and that you will find another companion, perhaps a better one. I wish you all the best, and good-bye."

He shook my hand and said: "Well, at least I am going to write to you, perhaps you will change your mind. Good-bye, and all the best."

When I got to that small railway station, the Niemelä girls were meeting me there, and happily we went to the house, where Mrs, Niemelä was waiting at the door to welcome me. She said: "Anni, you could not have picked a better time. Several men have already arrived and are waiting to get to the bunkhouse, and more are coming tomorrow. We must feed them all, and our girls have no experience of cooking yet. Besides they are so young," she added, "but when they get to be at least your age, they can help more; but already they can help with the dish washing and other chores. I am so tired." she said.

"Resting is excellent medicine for that, now why don't you sit down, Mrs. Niemelä."

(To be continued)

Episode 29, 12 Oct 1954

Then I called to little Esther: "My little friend, would you please bring me your mother's apron so I can start fixing supper at once. I'll get mine when we're done with the evening chores." Esther tied the apron around my waist, and at once I began to make a pie crust. And I did not need to ask where to find this or that, having helped out with the housekeeping here so many times before.

166

Mr. Niemelä came in with a couple of men and the eldest boy, Vilho. He gave me the widest and most mischievous smile, and said: "Hallo, Anni, it is good to have our 'daughter-in law' here". "Hallo, Mr. Niemelä" I said, blushing, and looked down at my work. Vilho came close to me and whispered: "How are you? Did you get away from the food house okay, Anni?" "Yes, I did," I replied.

There was plenty to do at the Niemelä farm in the countryside. All earth's bounty, product of so much hard work, had to be harvested for the coming winter. Mrs. Niemelä gave me the warmest welcome, saying: "Oh. It's so good you came, Anni. Now I can leave all the cooking to you and go about all the outdoor chores that I wouldn't have managed at all." I replied, "I am so glad for myself that I could come, and I am happy to do whatever I can. It is so much more fun to be in the country in the autumn than in town. But Mrs. Niemelä, of course you know that I have also another reason to rejoice, because Vilho is here!" After all Vilho and I had often made plans for the future, always with the same conclusion: one day when we grow up, or when we become of age..... At Niemelä, everyone worked hard all day long. When everything was finally harvested, even the turnip crop formed a pile as high as a haystack, and I had never seen so many turnips all at once in one place.

One morning, a team of sturdy horses pulled into the yard with half dozen young men in the carriage. One of the men who seemed to be slightly older than the others, stepped down and went to Mr. Niemelä. He asked whether they could stop and feed and rest their horses here overnight, as they were waiting for the rest of their crew to join them in the afternoon. Together, the whole crew would then go to a work site somewhere beyond the Niemalä property. An affable host, Mr. Niemelä welcomed them and came to the kitchen to say that we had company for lunch and yet more would be coming for supper, so make sure there will be enough food prepared.

I worked hard in the kitchen, with Lili helping me. Lunch went well. Late in the afternoon I was beginning preparations for supper, when Lili ran into the kitchen and said that the rest of the men were arriving now. I sat peeling potatoes when one of them came in, said good evening and asked for a drink of water. I got up to give him the water, with my cheeks blushing gently. The man went out again, and Lili began to tease me, saying: "Well, well, why are you blushing?" "Oh shush, stop kidding, it's just so hot in here," I said.

During the meal, the young men kept giving me sort of sideways glances, but I pretended not to notice. Right after the supper, the men went out of the house and into the old "bunkhouse" where mistress had readied several beds, also for those arriving the next day.

I sat with the family, exchanging news of our neighbors. I asked: "Has Father been here at the station recently?" They said that now that the road that went south past my home to a larger township and station and had been fixed up properly, my Father did not do business around here any longer.

Then the girls said that Maija, a neighbor's daughter, had come home for a visit, and as there were girls in other families, too, they decided to ask them all to come here on the following night; "If the men get back from work early enough then we can have a party in the large anteroom in the sauna building. Anni, you do remember all those games that mother and father said were played in Finland: "hiding the ring", "pawn", and many other fun games." "And we can include some of those games that we have learned at school in this country," said the youngest Niemelä girl.

Mr. and Mrs. Niemelä got excited about our plans, and they began to tell us about the games they had played in each of their home regions in Finland when they were young. Master told us how to play "Adam and Eves wedding". And mistress said that another fun game was the one in which the participant was told about the most beautiful sight they would ever see, and then, after certain introductory ceremonies, they are shown their own image in a mirror. She described this game in detail, so we would remember it on the following night.

Early on the following day the girls went and swept the large anteroom in the sauna house, and they brought in some logs on which they put long, planed planks as seats. I was too busy to go and see the preparations, because the first thing that morning, the mistress instructed me: "Anni, you better bake plenty of pies and pastries, so that there is enough for everyone; heaven knows how hungry the poor lads arriving will be, after a long journey."

So I began cooking supper very early, and I was standing at the counter with my hands covered in flour, when Esther came in and said: "Now there are at least three horse and carriage teams turning into our yard, with several men in each carriage." She went to peek out of the window, and when she saw that they were driving to the yard, she ran out, curious to hear what the men were talking about, because they were looking cheerful and not at all tired from their journey. I was nearly finished with potato peeling, when three handsome, straight backed young men stepped in; I responded to their"good evening" greetings and served them coffee as soon as I had put the potatoes in the kettle.

After the coffee, the boys went out to the others, to see to their horses, and Esther hurried in to tell me what the men had been talking about when she was listening nearby. She said that the handsome, shorter boy, who was the first to drive his horse to the yard, had asked the men who had arrived the previous day: "Are there any girls in the house?" And the others had said: "Yes, two grown-up girls, but one of them is already a daughter-in-law." Hearing this, the boy asking about girls had said: "They aren't married yet, are they?" "Well, no," the others had replied. Very amused, Esther said: "They must have meant you, Anni." Of course this amused me, too, and I said to Esther, you should not be so curious. The oldest daughter, Lilja, joined us and heard some of Esther's story, and so Esther had to tell her too what she had overheard.

After the supper we girls were hurrying to finish up washing the dishes, when Maija from next door came into the kitchen with some friends of hers. The men had already gone to the sauna house. The oldest daughter, pretty Lilja, was the perfect hostess for this occasion. She went in first and introduced us who came in after her to the young men, and like a real Master of Ceremonies she described the games that would kick off the evening. In many of the games, a

170

boy and a girl would be paired off, and I, by accident of course, was always paired with the same young man (his name was Erik), the one who had asked whether there were any girls in this house. Everyone was having a good time, and in the game that involved giving a "pawn" to someone, I had to give my wristwatch as a "pawn" to Erik. When the fun and games of the evening were over, the men had retired to their bunkhouse, and the neighbors' girls had gone home, Lilja and I stayed behind to tidy up in the anteroom. The family's son Vilho came in, grimly serious, and said to me: "What the devil was it with you tonight, Anni, why did you keep company with that stranger the whole night?" "You're talking nonsense, Vilho, it just happened, he kept guessing my number, and besides it was all just a coincidence, of course," I said.

"Oh it was, was it now," said Vilho, "didn't you Anni even give that Erik your wristwatch, and did he ever give it back?"

"Of course he did," I said and took my wristwatch from the pocket of my apron. Then Vilho began to calm down. He sat down on the sofa, and pulled me over to sit next to him. Then Lilja sat down on my other side, and began to chat about the games that had been played. She said, "Wasn't it funny how it took Erik so long to count the eyelets in your shoes, how he kept getting confused and had to start over?" "It's all rubbish," Vilho snapped angrily, "if that Erik is all you can talk about, I am going to bed." He got up and left, and Lilja and I sat there chatting a bit longer. Lilja asked: "If you had to choose one of those boys, which one would you pick?" I thought about it for a moment. Then I said: "Erik."

(To be continued)

Episode 30, 15 Oct 1954

Then my visit with the Niemelä family was over. I decided to go back to town and told Mrs. Niemelä about my decision. She asked me to stay on at least one more week, then suddenly she said:"I almost forgot, I have been asked to ask you to come and work just a few miles from here. Why not stay here, just think, wouldn't it be much nicer to spend the winter here than in town. You would have company too, as Vilho would be able to come and see you often." Against my will it occurred to me that Erik was somewhere nearby too. So, if I stayed here, perhaps I might also see him again some day. And so I stayed and started with great enthusiasm at my new place of work. Despite easy work, I missed the town life to which I was more used to. Neither Vilho's Sunday visits nor the many letters I got from my friends managed to lift my spirits. I also received several letters also from Niilo, but I never wrote back to him.

One night, I was sitting, holding a book in my hand, supposedly reading, but my thoughts were straying away from the contents of the book, when Master came into the kitchen and said: "There's a young man here who wants to see you, Anni, shall I ask him to come in?" "Sure," I replied casually, but when the visitor came in, I felt myself go first pale, then red, in turns. With great effort, I managed to reply when he said: "Good evening, Anni." I asked him to

172

take a seat, and after a while I overcame my astonishment and began chatting, and in the end we were talking like old friends.

As he was leaving, he asked if he could visit again, and pass time in my company in the long, cold winter nights. I said I had nothing against it, and when he visited again, we spent the evenings telling stories and singing. The family always joined in on our entertainments, seeing as, after all, we all belonged to the great family of the Finns. And I enjoyed much more working for a compatriot. It was almost like being related.

Once, when we were recalling songs again, Master asked: "Anni, can you sing the song 'Kultaisessa kartanossa'?" I said: "I learned it when I was little, I might still remember the melody."   And so I sang:

Kultaisessa kartanossa	In a golden manor
elää Ahti	lives Ahti
syvällä aalloissa.	deep under the waves.
Yö jo mustaan vaippahansa peittää,	With its dark veil the night covers the leaves,
lehdet, kukkaiset laaksoissa.	flowers in the valleys.

When I finished, Erik said: "I know a song that Anni likely doesn't know, but you can learn it, if you listen carefully." And Erik began to sing:

Yksi tähti taivaalla	A star in the sky

loisti niin kirkkasti,	was shining so bright,
jos sekään voisi kertoa	might it be able to tell
armaani missä on?	where my beloved is?

He sang it so beautifully. Then he sang the last verse:

Jos rikkaamman sä haluat	If you want someone richer
niin hylkää minut pois.	you must cast me aside.
Minä mielellään jään suremaan	I won't mind being left behind grieving
kun sinä vain onnen saat.	if only you find your happiness.

It brought tears to my eyes, and I stood up quickly, my excuse being that I had to put wood in the stove. I didn't want anyone to see my emotions. As I returned to the others, I was quite calm again, and I admitted that I really had not heard that song before. "But I'll learn it fast," I assured.

Vilho came to visit me again on Sunday night. He brought greetings from his sisters; and he said that his mother would like me to come and spend Christmas with them. Distracted, I just said: "It's still a long time until Christmas, and if everyone else goes away for Christmas, then of course I must stay here." He said: "That is not the real reason, Anni. You have changed altogether. Remember that we belong to each other." I considered his words for a moment. Then I said to Vilho: "Don't you remember what we decided? We promised not to marry until we turn twenty-one and even then only on the condition that by then we haven't changed our minds and found someone dearer. It's still a long time away." "Anni, you have changed, I don't understand you any longer. Can't you believe that my love will never change, no matter how old we may live? I hoped and believed that you felt the same way. I was certain that Father and Mother did not need to call you 'daughter-in-law' for nothing, that it would come true, in time. And it is what your Father has been hoping for, too, but now it seems that I can't be certain of anything," Vilho finished. As he left, he regretted that he would not be able to visit on the following Sunday, because he had to go on some trip with his Father, but "we'll meet again on another Sunday," he assured.

I stared after him, with mixed feelings, thinking that first love could not always be true as of course it was just "puppy love" that fades away when one comes to one's senses. I did not miss Vilho, because my thoughts were roaming elsewhere. Completely against my will I would look at the clock already around three in the afternoon, perhaps Erik will come for coffee in an hour's time. I pretended not to notice his arrival, though I had to admit to myself that day after another passed so sweetly simply because Erik was so near. We would spend the evenings chatting of this and that and the other thing, and the other young men would always join in on the conversation.

Once, the talk turned to fortune-telling. One after another the men described their experiences and their visits to fortune-tellers. One man said that he had had his fortune told from the cards, and nothing had come true so far. Another said that he had been to a fortune-teller who read the lines in one's palms, especially the "life lines". One or two things of the things he had been told had actually happened later. I was listening to their stories all quiet, and finally one of the men asked me: "Anni, have you ever been to a fortune-teller?" "Well, yes, once," I replied.

"You must tell us about it, Anni," came from several mouths, and I glanced at Erik who was just sitting there, as if he had not heard a single word. "How was it done, Anni, and what did the fortune-teller say?" one of the men asked. "The fortune-teller looked at my palm and told me so many things that I cannot possibly remember half of them. She said I would marry young, and my true life's companion will simply appear before me, the way Uusi Kotimaa used to, and that I shall have five children, but die young. Then she said that if I gave her another dollar, she would read my other palm, and give me a picture with the perfect likeness of my future husband. We were three girls in the fortune-teller's tent, and when I told them that she would read my other palm and give me a picture, they urged me to go ahead and pay her, and I was so stupid that I did, but I cannot remember what she said besides what she had already told me, I just took the picture that she chose among many in some odd looking box; I put it in my purse and left."

The men had been listening to my story, and now one of them asked: "Do you still have that picture, Anni?" "It must be in the box where I keep my letters," I replied. "In that case you just have to go and get it, so we may see it," they said, and I went to search for the picture, and I found it. About an inch and a half square it was, and not even all that clear.

The picture traveled from hand to hand, and finally also Erik took a look at it, and he gave me sort of a sideways glance, but to my annoyance, I blushed.

(To be continued)

Episode 31, 19 Oct 1954

The men began to ponder whether the picture resembled any of them. Then one of them asked: "Have you ever had your fortune told, Erik?" He said he had not. Another man said: "Where are the cards? I know a bit about reading cards. I'll read them for Erik." Someone brought the cards, and the man went to Erik, began to shuffle the cards. Then he asked Erik to cut the deck. I left them, supposedly for some chore or another, for I did not want to see or hear what the cards would tell Erik. They finished a while later, but one of the men came to me and said, "The cards said three times in a row that Erik will receive a letter from a young lady with blond hair, and we think it ought to come true. What do you say, Anni, Would you write a letter to Erik?" "Well for sure such a prediction must come true," I said. He brought me a piece of paper and a pen.

I wrote on the paper: "Erik, I like you a lot, truly, much more than anyone else" and I gave it to Erik. He read it slowly or perhaps twice, then he hurriedly put it in his pocket and said, almost serious: "This letter must be replied to." He took a pen and paper, wrote

177

a couple of words, folded the paper carefully, gave it to me and walked out of the door.

I put the paper in my apron pocket, without reading it, instead I began to clear the coffee cups off the table. I was amazed that none of the boys asked about the contents of the letters, or even teased me, as they usually would have.

Only much later, when I was alone in my room, did I take the slip of paper out of my apron pocket, and I read the following sentence: "You may be my beloved, if you truly love me." Love me, love me, the words kept echoing in my ears. I had written that I liked him a lot. I was wondering to myself whether it was one and the same thing.

I did not stay up all night to mull it over, but fell asleep quite easily. My employer, a widower, father of three children, had asked me several times, would I not marry him. He had promised to hire another cook at once, to build me a special room, and as the very first thing to get me the best silk dress that money could buy if I said yes. I just turned it all into play and said that my Father was exactly the same age as he was. In the end he stopped teasing me, and everyone else also seemed to have come to the understanding that Erik and I liked each other.

One morning Erik woke up with a bad tooth ache, and he went to the town to see the dentist. The afternoon train came and went, but Erik did not return. After supper the boys began to tease me: "Anni doesn't know where Erik is now, perhaps he has sweethearts in the town, and so he does not remember to come back." I said nothing, but I was still hoping that Erik would return before dawn. Just as I had finished setting the table for breakfast, there were sounds of snow being scraped off boots at the door, and Erik stepped in. His eyes were shining as he came to me and said: "Hallo, Anni, I missed the afternoon train, but the freight train left soon after, and I grabbed hold of the handles. There was freight to be unloaded at this station, so that made it easy, but was that train ever slow, I could almost have kept up with it by running alongside. I did not get any supper. Could you perhaps give me a cup of coffee and a sandwich?" I hurried to fix Erik something to eat, and at the same time I shot a haughty look at the boys sitting on the bench, even sneering a little.

The evenings were times of good fun, as everyone always had plenty to tell, especially because these men were from the same region in Finland, and some of them had arrived quite recently, so of course those who had been here longer had a lot of questions for them. One day, an older man, a friend of Erik's, came to visit, bringing greetings from their mutual friends. Then he turned to me, and said that a young man called Antti had asked him to bring his greetings to me, but I could not remember at once who this Antti was. Then the visitor said that Antti had said that he had met me in Vilho Niemelä's home, and that he would come and see me.

It was very seldom that Erik and I could sit together without anyone else being around, but sometimes no one happened to be close enough to overhear us. Those were the moments when Erik talked about himself and his home in Finland, how he had been orphaned when he was very little, and how his grandfather had raised him. He said his name was really Reino Erik Ahola, but here he had picked the more practical of the two first names. He was always so serious, and he said that if I liked him enough, I should forsake all others altogether. And he added: "It is your own business entirely, Anni. Leave Vilho and don't say a word to him when he comes round next Sunday. If you still keep him company, our relations are over." I tried to argue that not talking to someone is impolite. But he said he would leave the choice to me.

When Vilho came on that Sunday, it was fortunate that we had other visitors, too, so I managed to avoid talking to him. Vilho knew where I kept my writing materials. He had used them and written a long letter, placed it between the pages of a book, then he had put everything back in its place, and left. I knew nothing of it, as I had been serving the guests and talking to them, but the boys had kept a close eye on Vilho's doings. They had taken Vilho's letter and read it, then put it back where I would find it when I needed paper.

If anyone could write a beautiful love letter in Finnish, he certainly was one. There were even some verses:

Toivojeni määrä . unelmani	What I wish for, what I dream of
Öin ja päivin muistan sua	Night and day I think of you
Unissakin mua kuvas' pyhä	In my dreams the hallowed vision of you
seuraa yhä.	still haunts me
Maassa, taivahassa	In this world and in heaven
olet mun.	you are mine.

At the end, there was one more verse:

Mun olet	You are mine
vaikk' on maailma eroittanut.	though the world has separated us.
En ketään toista	No other
voi mä rakastaa.	could I ever love.
Sill' sama aatos	Because in my heart
rinnassani kaikui	there is but one thought
Mun olet vaan,	You are mine only,
mun oman' olet vaan.	my own, you are only mine.

    I did not say anything about this letter to Erik, and in the morning I burned the whole letter in the stove. But I could not help making comparisons and wondering which kind of love was more lasting; the burning, thrilling kind, or the serious, unwavering kind. All Erik had written was a couple of words: "You may be my beloved."

    Then Antti came to visit. He was all dressed up, gentleman style, so well that I nearly did not recognize him, which would not really have been any wonder at all, since I had only met him on that one occasion.

(To be continued)

Episode 32, 22 Oct 1954

He was working as some kind of an agent, and he was very well-mannered and social. While I was busy with my chores in the kitchen, the boys had already told him that Erik is Anni's friend. That night, when all the lads were there, they began to urge Antti to steal the girl away from Erik, and he said he had come here from the mill town of Cloquet for that very purpose. The next day, Antti tried in every possible way to change the subject to Erik, but I was pretending I was not even listening to him, and kept on chatting about other things. Finally he said right tauntingly: "Well, you don't even dare admit that you are Erik's girl friend." That made me mad and I said: "You listen to me, Antti, the way it is, I can admit at anytime that I am the girl friend of such a handsome and decent lad as Erik." That was all it took. Antti said his train was due soon, and he had to go. "Good-bye, Anni, and all the best," he said and rushed out of the door.

Then Erik wanted me to resign from my job, as he would take me to his friends. I resigned, and we went to the town. There he left me in a hotel. He promising to be back in a couple of hours, and he told me the time I should come and meet him at the station. I must have looked at the clock dozens of times when I stood waiting at the station, and I was beginning to think that I had been crazy to go with Erik. Suppose he is not coming. What shall I do then? I looked at the clock for one last time. Finally I went to see the station manager, and asked him whether that particular train had arrived. He said that the train was late due to unforeseeable reasons, but it would arrive any moment now. I let out a sigh of relief. The train arrived. I did not climb aboard. Instead I stood

182

waiting on top of the steps near the door of the station hall. Up the steps in hurried strides rushed a handsome man, so well dressed that I almost did not recognize him as Erik. He took me by the hand and said: "I was so afraid that you would get fed up with the waiting, and leave." My heart was beating so hard that I could not say a word. He led me out and said: "First we shall have a good meal, then we shall go and buy the rings, and after that I want to go and talk to your father."

That's when I recovered my ability to speak, and I said: "Well, I won't be taking you to see my Father, because he has said that in case I marry a man he does not like, he will shoot us both on the spot. So how could I possibly know whether or not he is going to like you Erik?"

So ended the discussion on that matter, and Erik took me to his friends' home. (Erik always stayed with them when he happened to be in town.) When we got there, they gave me such a friendly welcome. They said they knew me already, because Erik had told them about me while he had me waiting for him. This was where Erik had gotten dressed up, the way only a groom could. The mistress came to show me to my room, praising Erik's good qualities all the while. She said she had known Erik for a couple of years, and never once had she either seen or heard anything unseemly about Erik. The master said he would go with Erik to get the marriage license, and he asked which priest would we prefer to marry us. Erik asked: "Who are the priests around here nowadays?" When the master mentioned a particular Finnish priest, I was thrilled and said: "I know this priest, and his wife. Last summer they were in that small township where I was working for the Fords. And they came to the midsummer fest when I went there with the Ikola girls. I was introduced to them and the wife took such an interest in me that she wanted to spend the whole day with me. She was ever so kind, and she insisted that I should come for a long visit. Then she gave me detailed instructions on how to find them, and I promised to visit. I have thought about that priest and his kind wife so often, and now I would meet them again," I ended my speech.

The men left to run that momentous errand, while the mistress and her sisters began hurriedly organizing my wedding dress. Soon, dawned our wedding day. These friendly ladies dressed me up in a white gown, with white flowers in my hair, but the bouquet that Erik brought me was made of red roses.

A lively horse was waiting, harnessed to the church sleigh. Erik lifted me into the sleigh, sat down next to me and took the reins. We rode to the vicarage. Erik tied up the horse, but I was already rushing in, and the moment I opened the door, the vicar's wife came running to meet me and said, "Dear child, you remembered to come", and she embraced me. When I recovered enough from my astonishment and managed to say something, I asked: "Is the vicar at home" and at that moment Erik came in. I introduced him, and the vicar's wife said, "Yes, he is at home, but I think he went to the chicken coop". She went to the back door to take a look outside. Then apparently she saw the vicar coming, because she shouted, "Come, quickly, that young lady we met last summer at the midsummer fest is here now." The vicar came in, wearing overalls, as any farmer would. He shook our hands, and his wife introduced Erik to him, and Erik presented our business. The vicar said he would get changed, and in the meanwhile "mamma" would make some coffee. She was chatting how she had thought about me so often and how at first she had thought that now I had come to visit with them, but then she said, "Well, that's how life goes, and I am sure that you will be very happy." All I could think of to say was just, "Thank you."

Soon the wedding ceremony was over, and the vicar's wife had sung to us so beautifully, accompanying her singing on the organ. We left the vicarage followed by their best wishes. Everything had happened as if in a dream. At Erik's friends, a feast awaited us, but I cannot remember what I ate, or if I ate anything at all.

I began to say, "Shouldn't we start getting changed for the trip, Erik?" "Well let's not rush, 'Mrs Ahola', for first we must go to the photographer's in this getup, so that we can commemorate our grand day, and so that when you, Anni, have grown into an old woman, you can show the photo to our grandchildren and say, just you look at us, weren't we pretty back then, even though now we are but a pair of old 'wrinklies', grandma and grandpa." And Erik laughed so merrily at the end of his speech, but I went serious. I could not imagine life that far ahead.

After the photos had been taken and we were
returning to the Leppi house, Erik suddenly said: "In

that photo, the tie is exactly like the one in the picture in your purse."

"What are you talking about now?" I said, startled. "Well I am talking about that picture you got from that fortune teller. And, haven't you noticed that the picture sort of resembled me?" Erik asked. "It was a miracle that the other lads did not notice it, though they saw the picture first," he added. "Please, Erik, don't talk about it ever again," I asked.

Episode 33, 26 Oct 1954

"That fortune-telling was surely some of that great American 'humbug' with which they trick money out of silly fools such as for instance I am. The fortune teller said that I would die young, and I don't want to leave you a widower; I did see last night at the temperance hall how many a pretty young girl gazed at you with admiring eyes. Why, then I would die jealous, "young" as the fortune teller said." "That's it, then," said Erik. "You yourself said that we should talk no more about that fortune teller." "Well, let's not," I imitated.

We stayed with the Leppi family for one more day, because Erik had some errands to run. In the middle of the day, Mrs. Leppi's brother came home from work. He had hurt his finger and he said, "I should go and have a doctor look at it, but my English is so bad." I promised to interpret, and when we returned, with his finger seen to and properly bandaged, Mrs. Leppi began to tease her brother, saying, "My dear Veikko, you wouldn't have been so keen to take Anni with you, if you knew that she is now Mrs. Ahola." Veikko blushed but did not say anything. Antti had learned that Erik and I were at the Leppis', so he came calling, but before he made it to the front door from the hallway, Erik saw him coming and told Mrs. Leppi: "Antti is coming, tell him that we have gone out." He gave me my coat and said, "Put it on, we're going to the pictures" and he led me out through the back door.

I do not remember at all what picture it was, because our own life's serial had just begun. First thing in the morning we decided to go and visit my Father, and try to find a place to live and a job for Erik.

As we were saying our good-byes to the Leppi family and thanking them for everything, we had no idea that seven years later we would become neighbors.

We traveled to the township where I had been in the employment of the Ford family, and naturally the first thing we did was to go and visit the Ikolas. They were all ever so happy and everyone in their turn had plenty of questions. Teuto went and whispered to his mother that he could not believe that Anni was married. "Your father," Mrs. Ikola asked, "does your father know?" "Well, not yet," I said. "Oh, Anni, right now your father happens to be in our store. I just got home from the store, and I asked him to drop by for a cup of coffee," she said. I was so scared that my knees were trembling, and I looked Erik in the eye, but I did not see the least trace of fear, instead he returned my gaze with the honesty of an honest man. It gave me strength to bear whatever might happen.

There was no time to think of what I might do, as already there was a knock at the door. Mrs. Ikola went to open the door, and my Father came in. He said, "Good afternoon," then he saw me. I stood up, took

188

Erik by the hand, led him to my Father and introduced him. My Father looked at me, then at Erik. Then he said, "I see!" In that instant I could not tell whether it meant good or bad, then Mrs. Ikola quickly helped us out, saying, "Would everyone please be seated for the coffee." Tension eased.

My Father, like the gentleman he was, spoke politely and asked us to come with him to the farm, if we had nothing particular arranged just yet. Here Mrs. Ikola jumped in again, saying: "These youngsters have ordered some pieces of furniture through us, but it will take some time before they arrive." "Well in that case you should come and stay with us," said Father. We did.

My Father's wife welcomed us warmly. She seemed to like Erik at the very first sight, and she was chattering in her usual cheerful fashion. Erik went out for a look around the grounds, and when Father came in without him, he said that Erik had gone down to the lake. My Father's wife was in the kitchen, and now, that I was alone with my Father in the room, I was waiting with trepidation what Father would say, because I knew with certainty that he had been waiting for an opportunity such as this.

He began to speak and he said, "Erik does seem like a decent man, but why did you do this to me, Anni? Why didn't you come home and tell me first? I would have liked for you to get married here at home and for your uncle to officiate (my uncle was a priest). Surely all this must be Erik's doing and by his demand, isn't it, Anni?"

(To be continued)

Episode 34, 2 Nov 1954

"No, oh no Father, there isn't the least bit of blame in Erik, because when he gave me the engagement ring, he said, 'Now we must go and see your father at once.' But I said, 'We are not going there,' and then I told Erik how you, Father, once said that if I married someone you don't like, you will shoot us both on the spot." Father began to laugh, saying he had never said such a thing. I called to my Father's wife, and when she came from the kitchen, I asked her: "Do you remember my Father saying that?" She hesitated a bit at first, but then she said, all serious: "Yes, your father did say that." My Father was astonished. Then he tried to say: "Truly, I can't remember saying that, and anyway it was just a joke". "Why, even as a joke it was much too horrible, and I believed your words, so I could not know whether you would like Erik or not, and so I would not have dared to come and see you, if you had not by coincidence come to Ikola for coffee. Erik has been saying that he would see you right after the wedding, because I did not bring him to see you while we were engaged. And one more thing, I was afraid you would force me to give the engagement ring back to Erik, and accept Vilho's proposal, because you always wanted to have him for son-in-law."

Some time ago, my Father had received his naturalization documents, and, for good reason, he was very proud of them. Being a minor, I had of course become naturalized on his documents. Now I had lost my citizenship, because I had married an alien. (That was the law then.)

My Father began to tease me, saying I had

become an alien again, but I defended myself quite strongly, saying: "What use would a citizenship be to me now? Don't you remember that I shall remain a minor for a few more years, so even if I were a citizen, I would not be allowed to vote? Erik already has his first set of documents, and with time he will receive the second set. Then we shall both be full citizens, and we will be allowed to vote."

Erik wanted to go job hunting, and my Father suggested that I stay with them for a while. So Erik left, and I stayed with my Father. The first couple of days went easily, because my Father's wife was so sweet and we had so much to talk about.

She liked to reminisce about all kinds of past events. For example, one day, when I was a new arrival at my Father's farm, two men came to call. One was a short old man who spoke through his nose and the other was a young farmer, sturdy but painfully shy. My Father's wife knew both of them, but I didn't, and I was wondering why they had come. When they were leaving, after the coffee, the older man said: "The young lady of this household ought to come and marry this farmer, but reckon she won't, for now at least." They said good-bye and left. I stared at my Father's wife in utter amazement as she burst in gales of uncontrollable laughter, and I asked her: "What on earth did those men mean?" She said: "Well, it seems they were a groom and his spokesman, but they never got around to talking, and when they were leaving it was too late." Then she recalled another time when a young man had come calling. I chatted with him about this and that and the other thing. He had seemed to be in no hurry whatsoever to leave, which began to bother my Father an awful lot. He went out, apparently to chop some firewood, and he went about other such chores just outside the window, so I should understand to start sending the young man on his way, but I was pretending not to understand.

One day, a Saturday it was, I was weeding the vegetable patch, and my Father had already got the fire in the sauna stove started, so that a pillar of smoke was rising high from the chimney. Two young homestead fellows came to call, all dressed up in their Sunday clothes. They came and stood by the fence of the vegetable patch, greeted me, then asked: "What's the big rush that you must be weeding on a Sunday?" Then they saw the smoke rising from the sauna chimney, and they began to wonder: "Why, are you going to take a sauna bath today as well?" I laughed and said: "We always do on Saturdays." The lads would not believe that they had gotten the days of the week confused, but when my Father's wife assured them that it really was Saturday, they left, somewhat embarrassed, for their usual weekday chores. And she also recalled other similar stories from my first year in America. She told me that her sister's little girl who was born during my first summer in this country, with whose family I had been working as a nurse, was now a beautiful, healthy and lively girl.

"Well, then we must go and visit them," I said. We visited many other settlers, too, and a mile or two of walking did not seem like much of a distance at all. A couple of weeks went by quickly, but then a terrible longing struck me; and nothing could cheer me up. My Father had been to the town, and quite feverishly I had been waiting for a letter from Erik. I got nothing. For a moment I even suspected that my Father had kept the letter and did not give it to me, but I abandoned that thought, for he could not possibly be so cruel. He did tease me, saying that Erik must have forgotten that he is married, and he had left to see the world. Who knew where? I tried to keep my chin up, not wanting to show him how miserable I really was.

Then one of the neighbors dropped by, asking whether we needed anything from the town. He was planning to go the next morning, and I asked if I could go with him. "Well, Anni, of course you can come along," he said. It was a miracle that Father did not stop me. I spent the whole night awake, fretting, but in the morning I thought that if I could go and talk to Mrs. Ikola, surely I would feel better.

After thanking our neighbor for the ride, I rushed straight to the Ikola house, not stopping by the store at all. Mrs. Ikola happened to be alone in the house, and, crying, I ran into her open arms. She asked: "What's the matter? Has your Father been mean to you?" When I finally managed to speak from my sobbing, I said: "I haven't heard anything from Erik, and my Father says that he has left me and completely forgotten that he is married." "Why, what a foolish thing to say," said Mrs. Ikola. "Don't you see, Erik thought he was able to leave you in the safest possible place in the whole world, with your own Father, and so of course it has not occurred to him to write, that's how men are, most of the time. You just calm down now Anni my dear. He will come back as soon as he can. Oh but it is good that you came, I've got so much work here that I can't possibly get it all done, because Alma must mind the store and Hilma is in school in town. You can start right away with the ironing. There's a basket full of clothes, already sprinkled."

The youngest Ikola children came in. They were three-year old twins, Alli and Antti, and they asked at once: "Where is Erik?" The very first time I had come to Ikola with Erik, they had practically fallen in love with him. Erik had picked up the pair of them to sit on his knee, and Mrs. Ikola had been amazed to see them sitting on a stranger's knee, as they had never before gone near anyone new until they had slowly become acquainted with them.

(To be continued)

Episode 35, 5 Nov 1954

I tried to explain to the children that Erik was not there now, but maybe he would come soon. Then Mrs. Ikola said that only some of the furniture and supplies we had ordered had arrived so far, and should Erik be here by the time the rest arrived, we could start setting up our own home.

I began to feel more hopeful, and so I managed to sleep that night. We had the household in order by midday, and Mrs. Ikola poured us both a cup of coffee. We were sitting and sipping the coffee, when there was a knock at the door. Mrs. Ikola went to open the door, and there was Erik. He came in and was startled to see me. Then he quickly grabbed me into his arms and asked: "How come you're here? I was going to go straight to your home, then, I thought I might hear news of you here, in case your father has been to town." Mrs. Ikola quickly said: "Well, it's great

194

that you came here first. Anni came here with one of their neighbors. The poor child was so unhappy in the country, so I have been trying to console her." And Erik said: "You forgot your coffee", but I could not have swallowed a spoonful, I was all breathless and I had to hold back my tears. It was good that the twins came in just then, and ran straight into Erik's arms, so I could recover my balance.

Then Erik said that we would live here in town at least this summer. He had found work on the railroad, but he was planning to buy some land, only a couple of miles south of the town. We could go there when he was not working, and clear some land for a dwelling and a potato patch.

Mrs. Ikola came with us to see a house by the railroad. Erik got a truck and driver so we could move the furniture and supplies from the Ikola warehouse. Erik was laughing when he began to set up the bed. The ends, sides and mattress were there, but not the springs. He said that one could sleep on a mattress even on the floor, but it would be much worse to sleep on the springs without a mattress.

So we spent the first night in our own home, and then it took only a few days for the rest of the supplies to arrive. Every day seemed to end too early, there was always so much to do, so many chores one never thought of as the day dawned.

Then Father came to town, and when he came to see our new home, he seemed pleased, even though he did not say anything. I rushed to serve him a meal, and after that, every time he came to town, I always made him a good meal.

Once he said that his wife had begun to wonder how come he was no longer hungry when he got back home from town, and he had explained that he dines at his daughter's every time he goes to town.

The summer went quickly, and every weekend we went to the farm. We already had a small clearing, and enough logs for the walls of a one-room house. There were no roads, and in one place, near the boundary of our land, there was a swale where there was always water. Erik would set down his things, then he would carry me across the wet spot, then he would go back for our things. We would make coffee in a tin pot over a fire, and eat sandwiches we had brought with us. Erik said that he would soon cover that wet spot, and fix the road, so we could bring in the door, windows and roofing material for the room, and planks for a vestibule. We were brimming with enthusiasm and energy. It had not snowed yet when Erik quit his work on the railroad, and we were able to move to the country, into our own house. To earn money for our food, Erik began to cut timbers for railway sleepers, from our own woods.

I walked to the town for any smaller shopping needs. By now, the distance seemed so short, as Erik and I had walked it back and forth so often, but this time I was by myself. My first stop was the Ikola store. The Master said: "Well, Anni, it's been a while since we last saw you, why don't you go in and say hello to my wife." I did, and Mrs. Ikola asked me to take a seat, then she said: "You'll never guess who was here yesterday" . "I don't suppose I do, but you better tell me then, you are looking very mysterious," I replied. "Well, this visitor did not actually come to visit us, he was looking for you. He came to the store, asking if we knew where Erik and Anni Ahola lived. I told him that you used to live here in town, but that a while ago you moved to your own house in the country. When he learned that it's a couple of miles away, he said he had to go home that same night, so he did not have time to meet you now, but perhaps another time. But I did not leave him just standing there. I asked him to come in for a cup of coffee, and he was glad to come. When I asked him to sit down while I was setting the table, his eyes found your wedding photo on top of the piano. He took it in his hand, and he looked at it for a long time, and his face kept turning red and white in turns. I was pretending not to notice, and I busied myself by the stove. Finally he put the photo back on top of the piano, and I asked him his name. He said he was Vilho Niemelä, and he said he had known you Anni at the age of fourteen. He left as soon as he had drunk his coffee. And I can't help but wonder why on earth Anni did you leave such a handsome man. I mean, for sure Erik is a handsome man, too, but all in all that Vilho looked as if he had been created for you. You took the wrong man, dear Anni," finished Mrs. Ikola finally.

"Oh, please don't talk to me like that, Mrs. Ikola," I barely managed to say. "Aren't marriages tied in heaven?" I said good-bye to Mrs. Ikola and left for home, almost running. I had always considered Mrs. Ikola such a compassionate, well-intentioned woman, a true friend to me, and now she was talking like that. All the way home, I thought about her words, even cried bitterly. Finally I recovered my balance, feeling I regained my peace of mind when I thought about all those happy moments I had spent with Erik up to this day. I did not want to believe that Mrs. Ikola's words were more than idle talk, sheer and utter

197

nonsense. Briskly I walked home and promised myself
that I would forget the whole matter. It was just as well
that Erik was not at home, because for sure he would
have seen in my face how shocked I was.

I did not go to the town any more, because the
weather had turned colder, and Erik had gotten a
pair of horses for taking the timber to the town, so on
his return trip he was able to bring our small shopping
with him.

The winter was mild, and there was only little
snow. And then:

Tuuditin jo tupaseni ruusua	I was a-rocking the rose of my little home
Rakkauteni ensimmäistä kukkaa	The first bloom of my love
Mä lauloin, surut' on elämää	I sang, life is free of worries
Ei vaivojani elo vienyt hukkaan	My efforts have not been wasted

(To be continued)

Episode 36, 9 Nov 1954

Life to our tiny little baby boy did not look
promising. He weighed just a few pounds, and it was
hard to tell whether he was breathing at all unless you
put an ear right next to his face. He did not even cry.
He just slept. Erik looked worried and he said: "We'll
have him christened on Sunday. When I take the next
load to town, I'll go and ask your uncle to come and
christen our little boy." Two months went by, and the

baby did not seem to improve. Then one night he began to cry, and I didn't know what to do. Erik was tired from work, he had fallen asleep as soon as he got into bed, but I kept walking around, carrying the baby. He was not crying loudly, but the moment I stopped he would raise his voice. I walked back and forth, looking at the clock every now and then. It struck two, then three, finally four. That's when I got all upset and burst crying, too. I went to Erik, woke him up, and, through my tears, said something like: "You see to your brat!" Erik cradled the baby over his chest and said sleepily: "What, is our little man being mean to Mommy?" Then he began to hum softly, the baby stopped crying, and in a couple of minutes both father and son were fast asleep. I cried a little longer, whether out of frustration, or my own foolishness, I don't know. Finally I too fell asleep. From this moment on, the boy began to thrive quite noticeably.

Our home was close to Hilda's mother's house, and one day she dropped by, crooned to our boy, and chatted about this and that. Then she asked Erik whether he would haul some firewood to the town for her, now that she had a husband who had been cutting firewood.

I tried to intervene a bit, saying I reckoned Erik had no time to haul firewood for her, but Erik said he would do it. When she left, I said to Erik, that witch will never pay you your wage, but Erik who always trusted in people's honesty, said that surely she would pay him. (Today, the wage is still unpaid, and will remain so, for she died ages ago.)

In the spring, I went to town a couple of times. Then one day in July I visited the family for whom I used to work, the Fords. Their daughters had visited us every now and then, admiring our little baby boy. But now, as I went to the Fords', their oldest daughter came to the door, all excited, and said, almost stuttering: "Quickly, Anni, come in, come and see Mom's and Dad's baby." I did not quite understand what she meant, but found out soon, as she took me to my previous employer's room and showed me the baby sleeping in the cot.

The Fords had had a son, and their youngest daughter was nineteen years old. This certainly gave rise to plenty of talk in the town. Some people were saying that he must be the daughter's baby, yet oddly the mother was the one in childbed. I might have thought so, too, but that day I saw both daughters, and the whole family.

After this, the Ford girls became very friendly with me because our son was six months old when their baby brother was born. They had lots of questions, on every possible aspect: when did our baby get his first tooth, was it up or down, when did he sit up on his own, when did he start crawling, and so on. Based on my answers they tried and calculate when their baby brother would be doing those same things.

Then times of suffering came upon us. My Father got horribly angry over some issue that I cannot recall. He threatened to separate us on the grounds of my getting married as a minor, without his permission, and he demanded that I come back home. This of course upset Erik terribly, and he said some hurtful things because he thought that I was defending my Father. Finally I wrote to my Father, but I no longer remember what I wrote. Our relations, both good and bad, got severed then. We did not see each other at all for years, but later, when I really thought about it, I am pretty sure we owed it to my good stepmother. Surely it was she who helped my Father understand that we should be left in peace.

We had been living in the country for a year. Erik realized that this land could never be cleared into fields, as the whole area was covered with stands of large maple and oak. Because just cutting firewood was not enough for a living, he decided to claim a homestead.

PART V: HOMESTEAD LIFE, EPISODES 36-52

I want to begin this part with the words of our great poet, J. L. Runeberg:

Mennyttä aikaa muistelen	I recall bygone days
Niin mielelläni vielä	with such great pleasure
Niin moni armas tähtönen	So many a beloved star
Minulle viittaa siellä	twinkles at me there
Ken mua seuraa retkellen	Who will accompany me on my trip

Not to the shores of Lake Näsijärvi, but to the shores of our homestead lake. We had decided to become homesteaders and settle deep in the heartlands. We did not even wait for spring. We took off in the winter when snow drifts were still high, for we had heard that near our property a small hut was standing empty. It would shelter us while we built our own cabin. We would have to travel by ski, across unpopulated land and impassable roads. Nowadays I cannot help wondering how much daring and self confidence one possesses in the days of ones youth.

We set off on ski, when the snow drifts were still high. Erik went first, with our son, I brought up the rear. During my school years in Finland I had considered myself a good skier, but this skiing was exhausting. Finally we reached the cabin of a man who lived there alone, and there we had to stay for a couple of days. Our things were brought in later, and we were able to settle in an empty cabin, only half a mile away from our homestead land.

We had to give up our pair of horses for the benefit of my Father, and we had to start empty-handed. When the snow drifts became lower, Erik began to fell timbers for the house. Every once in a while he had to go and work elsewhere for money, or we would not have had food. All food supplies had also been brought in when there was still snow, because in summer one had to go by foot, so heavy loads were impossible to transport. And in between all other busy work, one had to find time for road clearing. But the sheer amount of work did not daunt us, for we were brimming with the vigor of youth and strength. Even any and all obstacles seemed a mere trifling. Here in the heartlands, nature was fabulously beautiful. If you went out early in the morning in springtime, you could hear sounds made by many different wild animals. You might see a doe and her fawn make their way freely along the forest paths. Occasionally one saw moose crowned by large antlers, and black bear were also a common sight. Wolves, however, did not show themselves although their chilling howling could often be heard at night.

Spring seemed to be coming early. I began to hoe the ground and set up a small vegetable patch near the cabin. Erik had managed to buy a cow, and we housed her in the small cabin. She came home every morning and night, so we had milk, but one night she ran home, trembling and out of breath, and she gave very little milk. She did not roam very far the next day, nor the next few weeks. We believed that she had been bothered by a bear. After a while, though, she began to produce more milk.

Visitors did not drop by very often, but one day an Indian woman walked to the yard, and watched me work on my vegetable patch. I asked her in, and told her to take a seat while I made us some coffee. On the table, there was a big bowl full of sugar cubes, and some other bowl, but I saw that the water bucket was empty. I said to her: "Please wait a moment, I'll make the coffee at once, but first I must go get some water from the spring. I'll be right back." I ran to the spring and back, but when I was nearing the house, I saw the Indian woman run away fast, holding her skirts bundled up in front of her. I was wondering what had happened to make her run off, holding her skirts like that. I went in and set down the water bucket. I was panting and so out of breath, having rushed to get the coffee made quickly.

(To be continued)

Episode 37, 12 Nov 1954

My gaze stopped at the table. The sugar bowl was empty. That darned woman had poured all my sugar cubes into her bundled skirts and then scurried off.

The spring seemed to be so full of hope, but then, on the first of May, the weather suddenly turned terribly cold. It began to snow so heavily that at least three feet fell on the ground. It made me awfully sad to see so many small birds lifeless and frozen in the snow. When I went to check on the cow, the hut was crowded with little birds that flew out of the door in such a rush that I had to protect my eyes. I left the door ajar so that the poor birds could go and shelter in the hut again.

When I went in and told Erik about it, he said: "Guess what, this snow is a blessing in disguise." Already pulling on his overcoat and hat he said "I'll go and see our neighbor at once, and borrow his horse and "kuutti", so I can go and size the largest logs for our house. It'll make work easier for me, and even speed up building." It made me so happy that Erik always found some cause of joy in everything, and so I began to sing:

Nytpä tahdon olla mä	Now I want to become
pienen mökin laittaja.	the builder of a small cabin.
Seinät kun saan valmihiksi,	As soon as the walls are up,
toisen pään teen kammariksi	one end shall be the bedroom
Päähän toiseen pirttisen,	The other end shall be the kitchen
sievän, hauskan, puhtoisen.	pretty, nice and clean.

It is easy to sing about all such building activities, but the actual work takes a lot of time. Especially when the work continues just like the song tells:

Sitten vielä rakennan	Then I shall also build
tallin, aitan, navetan.	a stable, barn and cowshed
Hyv' on olla myöskin sauna,	It's also good to have a sauna house
jossa kylven lauantaina.	where I'll bathe on Saturdays.
Riihi metsän rinnassa,	A drying barn near the forest,
nuottakota rannalla.	a boat house on

208

the shore.

This was the spring of 1909. Snow melted, and summer set in with full force. Everything seemed to be growing fast. My small vegetable patch was veritably flourishing. I had kept the seed potatoes in the cabin so they had sprouted well, and when I planted them, they grew so fast that on Independence Day, we were able to feast on new potato, and cabbage as well.

Erik decided to go and work in town for a while, but he had to stay there a week at a time. As he could come home only on weekends, he fretted about leaving me alone for such long periods of time. I was brave, saying I had little Erik cheering me up, but Erik wanted to go and get me a companion, a young girl from a large family two miles away. I tried to stop him, but in the morning he just went and brought her back with him, then he left for town. I tried to act cheerful as he was leaving, but could not help feeling so unhappy that I had to hold back my tears.

The girl sat still for a while, but then she began scratching her scalp. I asked her, "Do you have head lice"? She said "Yes". I took a chair out in the yard, and got a fine-toothed comb. Then I told her to sit down, and I started combing her hair. She had big, beautiful hair, but so teeming with lice that I just dropped them off the comb and buried them in the dirt. Then I got some lamp oil, rubbed it into her scalp and hair and wrapped her hair and head in a piece of cloth. "Reckon you've got vermin in your clothes too", I said and got her some of my own clothes to wear. Then I took all her clothes, put them in the laundry cauldron that was placed over some stones in the yard, poured in water and soap, and lit a roaring fire under the cauldron. After I had washed and combed her hair a few more times, we were rid of the vermin. Then we cried together: I cried for the poor girl's misery, but I could not tell why she was crying.

A couple of weeks of working in the town helped a lot, and Erik was able to get windows and other things. He made the roofing shingles himself.

Autumn was already on its way, and finally, on October 1, we were able to move into our own home. I will never forget that memorable moment, for we had worked towards it with all the vigor of our youth. Early in the autumn I had found berries and made jam. Erik had shot a deer. The meat was carefully cleaned and salted. Then the container was placed into a deep hole in the ground, with a lid and a heavy weight on top. Back in those days, one was allowed to shoot two deer and one moose on one hunting license. So, there was no shortage of meat because there was no restrictions on storage time of game as there are now.

I returned to the little cabin to move all the plants to our new home, but when I got there, the fence was broken, and all the plants had been torn and chewed into bits and pieces. It was amazing, animals must have come from far away and wreaked this destruction, yet while we lived there we never saw any strange cattle around.

I have forgotten to mention that besides that Indian woman, we did have another visitor, right before we moved into our new home. It was Vilho Niemelä. He said he was surveying the woods, and he had come by our cabin purely by accident. He said he too was married now. He said that he had married the first girl he had happened to see. He claimed that after another man had stolen his girl, it no longer mattered whom he married.

There had been a time when I believed that I could never forget Vilho, but I truly had forgotten him completely, and now it felt awkward to see him, by accident or otherwise.

We had lived in our new home for no more than two weeks when our second heir was born, a daughter. Before the baby was born, we had always called it Pekka. Now it was hard to remember that the baby was a girl, and the name Pekka stuck as her nickname.

One day, two men on their forest surveying trip dropped by. They came in, and they asked the children's names, and I said: "Erik and Pekka". "So you have two boys," said one of the men. "No, the youngest is a girl," I said, blushing up to my ears.

When our baby girl was a week or two of age, Erik accidentally hit himself in the knee with an axe. When he came in and I saw what had happened, I was terribly frightened. He said, don't you worry, Anni, I brought some medicine for it, and he handed me some balsam fir bark. It had lots of little bumps, almost like blisters. We washed the wound well and then Erik punctured some of those blisters and dropped plenty of resin on the wound. Then we dressed the wound. I told him to settle on the bed. He assured me that the balsam resin would heal the wound fast, but the wound began to hurt, and Erik could not use that leg at all. Erik began to get worried, saying that we were supposed to notify the authorities of the birth of our daughter within ten days, and now he could not even walk. The first snow had fallen on the night our daughter was born. The cow had not come home by herself but Erik had found her and now we did not let her out any longer, and she was giving very little milk. By now, the first snow had melted, but it was very wet. Bravely I told Erik not to worry. I will make a note of our daughter's birth, and take the note to our neighbors, so they'll take it to the authorities on their next trip to town. Erik tried to stop me, but I just said, I'm young, so what's a couple of miles of walking. And I did not want to think about the fact that I was mother to an eight-day-old baby. When I was at the door, Erik was still trying to stop me, saying, let them fine us, don't go Anni. I left and ran the errand, but when I got back I was totally exhausted.

(To be continued)

Episode 38, 19 Nov 1954

Erik's leg kept on aching, and it seemed to be getting worse. We were both beginning to worry. We were running low on food supplies, but we still had meat. Erik said he still had some wages owing to him in the town, but what good was it now when he could not even walk.

This continued for a couple of weeks. Then, one Sunday, visitors arrived, and they did not come empty-handed. In late October, the weather had miraculously turned beautiful, and our guests said that the beautiful weather had inspired them to come and visit us. My uncle the priest came, too, and he said, as there is a newborn in the house, and guests fit for godparents, let's make this a christening day. "Pekka" was christened Maria, and with the food they

212

had brought the guests laid out a veritable feast.

The guests did not say a single word of our distressed circumstances. The ladies told me to sit down, saying they wanted to play hostess for us for the day. That day became such a cherished memory for us. After our guests had gone, I said to Erik: "They must have heard about us when the neighbor took the note of our baby to the officials in town. Surely they did not come to call just because this beautiful Indian summer inspired them, no matter what they said." "Yes, so it would seem," Erik said, thoughtfully, "but for sure poverty will flee as soon as my leg heals." And truly it was the only time in our homestead life that we were fraught with poverty.

Erik went out hunting, so we had meat. Then he went to a remote mountain lake to shoot water fowl, and he came home with a heavy load. Starting with that very first catch, I gathered all the pretty feathers, and every time thereafter, and finally we had enough to stuff all of the pillows in our house. In those days, there were not many hunters around yet, so there were plenty of different game birds, especially on the small lakes deep in the wilderness. We could not possibly eat all the meat all that quickly, so I cleaned the meat and put it in a large stone pot with some salt. Thus the meat kept well during cold weather.

I too, fancied learning the noble art of hunting. I decided to try my luck at setting traps for rabbits which in those days were large and free from disease. Every now and then I also caught a spruce-grouse, or a partridge. Then Erik taught me to trap weasel, and I was ever so proud when I brought home my first weasel. After that I caught many more and Erik skinned them and tacked the hides to boards to dry, and he said: "Anni, you may keep all the money from the weasel skins." At once I began to think about all the things I could buy us for Christmas with the weasel skin money.

One morning I was checking my traps, and there was a great big hawk in one of them. I took a large piece of wood and tried to hit it, but it just kept hissing and lunging at me. I did not dare do anything else, instead I ran home, and Erik went and released the hawk from the trap. It had a broken leg, so it had to be put down. That hawk sure was a big one.

Then the news reached us that quite soon a large logging operation would start up only some three miles away from our home, and they had already started building bunkhouses. Erik went to take a look, and he was promised work as soon as the bunkhouses were finished and roads were cleared. Erik was ever so pleased to have work all arranged for the winter. With great vigor, he began to chop firewood, saying he'll chop now as much as possible, and in the winter we can make some more on Sundays. Some time earlier, I had learned to saw a bit, as every now and then Erik had asked me to man one end of the long saw when he was cutting large trees. I thought I was a pretty good hand at sawing, then one day Erik said: "Look, Anni, I don't care if you lean over the saw but for goodness' sake, don't drag your feet." It was like a slap in the face. I tried to learn to saw lighter, and some time later I overheard Erik telling the neighbor's son: "Anni is now a pretty good hand at sawing."

When the winter set in with all its ways, we had a warm house and plenty of food. Erik left for his work at the logging camp, and I missed him very much,

214

though I tried to busy myself endlessly with all kinds of chores. Early in the week I consoled myself with the thought that he had been home on Sunday, and towards the end of the week I began to look forward to his imminent return.   All day Saturday I cooked all kinds of his favorite foods, and kept water boiling on the stove so I could make coffee as soon as he arrived. I would feed and bathe the children and put them to bed. Then I would stay up waiting for Erik's arrival. There is a saying: "Time goes by so slowly for those who wait", and is it ever true. Finally the wait was over and Erik came in. He took off his outer clothes and I asked him: "What would you like first, Erik? There's boiling water for coffee."

He said: "I'm just going to sit down and take a moment's breather; you come here and sit on my knee, Anni". Then he asked how we had been, and after I told him, he said: "Now you can go and make that coffee." Then he described the life in the bunkhouses, and he said: "Lots of men would like to have homemade socks, would you Anni like to start knitting socks now that you can't go trapping any longer?" "Why, that'll be both pleasure and business for me," I said, delighted. "Bring me wool the next time you come home."

The bunkhouse boss usually brought also my food supplies from town, based on the list I gave Erik, and Erik brought the supplies to me on Saturdays. Once, the boss returned from town so late that Erik had already come home. I said to Erik: "It's a happy accident, now you stay home on your day off, while I take your skis, ski out to the camp and bring the supplies home in your backpack."

That Sunday, the weather was beautiful and

conditions were good for skiing. It felt good to get out of the house. Gliding along in a familiar, easy fashion, happy and carefree, I sang:

...ulos sukset survaiskaa!   ..bring out your skis!

Lumi peittää laaksot vouret...   snow covers all valleys and mountains

Erik's ski tracks were so clear that there was no danger of getting lost, though I had to cross a wide open marsh where only a few blackened tree stumps were sticking out here and there, not yet fully covered with snow. When I reached the bunkhouse, I took a short rest, and had a nice chat, too, as I knew the woman who was working as the cook there. When I left for home, the sky had turned dark and a harsh wind began to blow. I tried to hurry, but already the wind was making my progress difficult. When I was well on my way across the marsh, I stumbled. One ski came off, and the wind began to drive it forward. I was so terribly frightened. With one ski, I tried to go fast and catch the other, but suddenly I came to a full stop and yelped in terror. Was that a bear near the runaway ski? I looked and looked, and thought I saw something move there. I cannot possibly describe those feelings of horror. Screaming would have been useless. I must go on, I thought. Then all of a sudden I remembered that bears were not awake and about in the middle of winter. I tried to take one more, hard look and the dark shape was not moving after all. It was just one of those black stumps I had seen on my way to the camp. The stump had burned and so

216

formed this odd shape, that from this angle, looked like an animal. On its other side however, the one I saw on my way to the logging camp, was so entirely different that I had not really noticed it at all.

But it was far away now. I had lost Erik's ski tracks. Oh, what a fool I am, I thought, but I still had a long way home. The tree tops at the opposite end of the marsh could help me determine where I should be headed, as one pine was much taller than the others, and that's where Erik's ski tracks were.

(To be continued)

Episode 39, 23 Nov 1954

Having finally wrestled my ski from the grip of the winds, I put it back on, and resumed my trip homeward, beginning to feel more settled already. But my trials were not over yet. The homeward edge of the marsh, where a thick stand of alders grew, was no longer that far away. I was skiing, out of breath, and the pack on my back was feeling much too heavy. Then, quite near, behind the alder thicket, I heard loud bellowing. It almost froze my blood; it was a terrible sound, and it was close. I knew that it was a big moose. Not long ago, the lumberjacks had shot its mate, now it was angry and it could smell me in the side wind. As I mustered my remaining strength in order to cross the marsh, I could still hear angry mooing, but I was hoping that the moose would not come to the dry ground.

When I got home, I was so exhausted that I could not even speak. I just burst into floods of tears. When I calmed down, I told Erik about my adventure. I

217

expected him to laugh at me, and mock me, but he did neither, instead he said, very serious, that he was sorry he had let me go, but he had not guessed that the weather would turn so quickly, as it was so beautiful in the morning. He had hoped that I would enjoy having a chance to chat with the bunkhouse cook, as I had not seen another woman for months. Later Erik went to look at the place where I said I heard the bellowing and he found the tracks of a large moose.

Then I told Erik that the bunkhouse boss had asked me to join them for a meal, inquiring whether Mrs. Ahola dared to eat bear meat, because not all the men in the bunkhouse did. I looked at the cook's face and realized at once what was going on, and so I replied to the boss, why, of course I did, and having finished my meal, I said that it sure was good. Erik asked: "Did you know it was moose meat?" I said: "The cook whispered it to me before the meal."

That winter, skiing skills would have been greatly valuable for another reason too, in my opinion. Women were given the right to vote in this country. But it was only your father who got to ski to the voting place across the marshes and bogs. To my annoyance, I had to settle for skiing out to check my traps.

So passed the winter, and we managed to store some food supplies, especially the heavier kind, so that Erik did not have to carry them in the summer, as that was the only possible mode of transportation. Whenever he had time, he cut down trees to make a road, but in two places one had to cross the marsh to reach the main road. One had to chop trees for those spots, and it took time and effort. In the winter, the

218

marshes froze over, so traveling was easier.

In the logging camp, work went on also in the summer, but Erik came home so that we could start making fields. We were so happy that the soil here was not rocky at all. We took our spades, and side by side we turned the soil which was dark and sweet-smelling. The amount of work did not intimidate us, for we were young and full of vigor and energy. Even any and all obstacles seemed insignificant. The nature was fabulously beautiful, we did not long for the joys of the life in town, nor did we miss other people's company. We finished our fields. However we could not sow anything, because heavy rains set in. I had already begun to soak corn seeds to make them sprout better, and they did sprout, but it just kept on raining. I had to get a wood box, and I put the seeds in the box and covered them with soil. They began to shoot. First they grew one leaf, then another, then a third.

We decided, let it rain, we will plant the corn regardless. We put on raincoats and went to the field with the box of corn sprouts, and so we planted them. The soil contained no clay, and though it was so wet, it did not stick to the boots or tools, so with some effort, we managed to plant the sprouts. We sure got soaking wet, but we were happy because we had achieved something.

When the rains finally ceased we were able to finish the rest of the planting, and Erik went back to work in the logging camp. When he came home at the end of the week, he began to hew a boat out of a large pine which was dry and hollow inside, and it took him no time at all to get the boat done. A straight board was nailed tight at the stern, two boards in the front to form a wedge, and a seat in the middle. He made the oars out of dry lumber, but the oarlocks he had to get from town. When we set the boat afloat in the lake, we had the most wonderful time because the lake was teeming with fish. Erik dropped the anchor so that the boat stayed in one place, then he began angling. The only kind of fish we caught there was perch, but they were big and beautiful. Erik gave me very specific instructions on how to put the boat in the water, where to row, and how to cast the anchor, with one end of its line tightly secured to the boat. He also showed me where in the boat I should seat the children when I went out fishing with them.

Thus it was with great anticipation that I looked forward to the first Monday after Erik's return to the logging camp, so I could take the children out fishing on our lake. Erik told me to take a piece of pork meat and use it as my first bait, then cut a piece of the first-caught fish and use that as bait for the other fish. He also told me to take a bucket and put the fish in it.

That Monday morning I did my morning chores right fast and mechanically. The weather was calm and beautiful. I dressed the children carefully, telling them: "Now you're going fishing with Mommy." On one arm, I arranged our baby girl (she did not walk yet) and the bucket, and with my other hand, I led little Erik. Erik had left the fishing gear in the boat for us.

When we got to the boat, I seated the children on the bottom in the middle of the boat, pushed the boat afloat, and rowed to the designated spot. The anchor went down with a great big splash. I began angling, and I pulled up one fish after another, as soon I got them off the hook. Once the bait dropped off while the line was still in the air, but I let the hook sink in the water anyway, and a perch got stuck on it by its side. In no time, there were so many fish in the bucket that it was getting heavy to carry. The children had been sitting still the whole time, and happily I rowed back to the shore. I walked home with my heavy load, pleased that we now had plenty of fish to add to our meals. It was only after I had taken a brief rest and fed the children that a thought occurred to me: suppose the boat had capsized; there would have been absolutely nobody coming to our rescue, and screaming for help would have been useless. I felt quite faint just thinking about this possibility, but I believed in "Providence", nothing would happen to us.

Later, I made many more fishing trips and always with good luck. Nobody had ever fished that lake before, because it was in the middle of the uncharted wilderness. (It was not until several years later that a state land surveyor happened on that lake, and he gave it our name, and even today that name is still marked on the maps.)

Some nights, when there was a beautiful moonlight, I put the children to bed and slipped out quietly. I knew that our neighbor had been to town and brought both of our mail, so I decided to go get ours. The distance from our house to theirs was only some two miles but I could halve it by rowing across the lake.

I ran to the shore, pushed the boat into the water and rowed as fast as I could to the opposite side of the lake. Then I walked up to the neighbor's house, knowing they had brought our mail from town. I had no time to stay for the coffee they offered. Instead I took off running, carrying our mail under one arm. Back on our home shore, I broke into a run again, towards home, but my heart was beating so hard that I felt fit to choke. Suppose the children had woken up, or something had happened. I was almost scared to open the door, but I found the children fast asleep, in the exact same position as when I had left. With a great sigh of relief, I collapsed on the chair. Bursting into tears, I swore that I would never leave my babies alone again, no matter what errand needed doing. Keeping that promise however, was of course an entirely different thing.

(To be continued)

Episode 40, 30 Nov 1954

Nothing would do but I had to leave the children home alone again, because the cows got troublesome and did not come home by themselves. One had to go and get them. One day, when I was walking around in the woods, wearing a white headscarf, a great big hawk began to follow me around. I was running back and forth in the sparse brush, but the hawk just kept on following me, swooping down so near my head that I cried out in terror. I ran hard and made it into some thicker bush, and there I stayed for a while, to see if the hawk was still after me, but now it was gone. Now I had a new problem: to figure out where my running had taken me. There was no doubt that I was lost.

I was thinking and listening. I began to hear faraway cow bells and took off towards the sound in a hurry. Panting and exhausted I reached the cows and began to drive them home, but upon seeing me they

222

took off running, in what I believed to be a totally wrong direction. I was so scared, but I decided to follow the cows, no matter where they went, because I did not know the right direction myself, I was totally confused and lost. The cows went on running, and I was running and following them. Finally they stopped at the home gate, looking backwards at me who almost did not recognize our own gate.

Some time after that, I decided again to go get our mail, but not by boat, by foot instead, walking along the paths, or, half running, really. It was not dark yet, and I was sure I would get back home before dark. The children were sleeping, and I was certain that they would not wake up while I was gone. I was not worried, I just sang:

Tähtinen taivas ja kuutamoyö	Starry skies and a moonlit night
tien viittana kulkurin on.	are a wanderer's road signs.
Jos kuinkakin matkalla kiristää vyö	Whenever my belt gets tighter
taas poikkean mä talohon.	I shall drop by a house on my way.

I had no time to chat with the neighbor's friendly wife. I just took my mail and said I had to hurry because I left the children home alone, asleep. On the way back, I no longer felt like singing. I was terribly frightened. All sorts of thoughts came into my mind: suppose the children had awoken and seen that I was not at home, and they had wandered out, looking for me. I ran, and when I looked in the direction of our home, I saw red flames there. I screamed, our home is on fire. My knees turned into soft wax. I fell on the ground. I could not move a single limb. I had passed out for a moment. With great effort, I stood up and looked in the same direction. The moon had just cleared the tops of the trees. Just a moment earlier, it had been glowing between the trees, and I had believed it was a house fire. At home, all was calm, but I could not stop shaking.

It was hard to believe that it was just the moon. That sight left such a terrible scar in my mind that even today, decades later, I can still recall it when I see a full moon rising behind the trees. Even today it still resembles a blazing fire, if its outline is not visible.

Our small vegetable patch was our great pride and joy. Everything we planted grew well in the new, rich soil. Erik said it would be wise to clear land so we could grow grain crops next year. I did not say anything, but earlier I had made plans to go and chop down some bushes, away from the house. There was a pretty spot with no trees standing, only one or two fallen trees. I decided to leave some dense bushes standing between the house and that spot, and make a small clearing. Nobody would see me breaking off branches there. I brought a large blanket on which the children could sit and play. Oh, how I made quick progress, and the piles of branches and twigs grew higher and higher. When the children grew restless, I took them in the house, fed them and put them to bed. I had not yet changed into my housecoat, or even taken off Erik's big boots, when there was a knock on the door. I went to open the door, and there was my Father. He said, good day! And then he spoke the familiar "Right." I asked him to

224

take a seat and made some coffee quickly. He said he had come to see some woodland, and he wanted to speak to the bunkhouse boss, so, passing by, he dropped in on us. He did not ask anything, and after the cup of coffee, he went on his way.

I remained sitting there, feeling very confused. I remembered past times, how close my Father and I had been when I was a child, at home. He had been much closer and dearer to me than Mother. Father had always taken care of me, he even saw to my school clothes. He always ordered them himself, even my shoes. I sat there for a moment longer. Erik came home and said he had quit logging for a while. It was almost hay making time. I told him that my Father had just stopped by, on his way to survey some piece of woodland. Erik gave me a long look. Finally he said: "And is that what you were wearing when your Father came?" I said: "Yeah, I had not had any time to change yet, I had been out clearing some bushland, and I had to see to the children first." "And you were wearing those shoes, weren't you"?

"Yes," I admitted quietly. That made Erik raging mad and said: "What do you suppose your Father is thinking now? He must believe that you don't even have any shoes of your own or decent clothes"! Erik was boiling mad. He said that my Father had never approved of our marriage no matter how friendly he seemed at first. And what on earth must he be thinking now, or saying. I burst crying, and tried to defend myself, saying I did not think Father had paid any attention whatsoever to whether I was wearing shoes or not.

That was the end of that discussion. Erik went about his chores in the yard, and I began to scrub the

225

floor. I had scrubbed more than half the floor, when Erik came in and said: "Little Mom, you're working too hard, don't wear yourself out!" I burst crying again, saying: "Why do you take pity on me now, Erik, after that scolding you just gave me."

He had already forgotten his burst of anger. He always did. He would flare out mindlessly and then calm down in no time. I, on the other hand, would stew and simmer in the sulks, as Erik used to say.

Hay making time was ahead. Hay seemed to be growing everywhere, but Erik said he would go to the other side of the marsh to mow hay. There was a large clearing with no trees or obstacles, covered in the tall wild hay they called "red top". Erik named the clearing "Liminka", and he piled up several big hay stacks there. He said he would mow hay near the house only enough to last until the marsh froze over and he could haul the red-top hay home. When he had dry hay near the house, he told me to come and pile up the hay on the stack. We seated the children nearby. However, when I got on top of the haystack, I was useless. I just never managed to pile the hay in the way Erik wanted. I was scared that he would get mad, but he just told me to climb down and said: "Little Mom, you better go home."

I climbed down, took the children home, then made some coffee and took it, running, to Erik. I was wondering what he might say, but he did not say a word, nor did he ever speak of hay making again. Thus ended my efforts at hay making short and fast.

One cloudy day, Erik decided to go to town, to get us some food supplies and our mail, and also, in our turn, the neighbors' mail.

(To be continued)

Episode 41, 3 Dec 1954

When he got back home, he said he had visited the Ikolas, as Mrs. Ikola had asked him in for a cup of coffee. She had given him all kinds of latest local news, or should I say gossip. Among other things I heard that my former employer Mr. Ford's childhood sweetheart, of whom I have written earlier, had fallen sick, and Mr. Ford had once again sent her to the hospital. This had happened several times. It already was a public secret when I was employed by the Fords. This time, the doctor could no longer save her life. That stunningly beautiful lady had to move to the mansions of Tuoni, and her body had been brought to the town church for the burial.

Mr. Ford had been ailing due to a heart condition, and the doctors had warned him and told him to avoid any and all emotional turmoil. Now he was torn over whether or not to go to the church to view his one and only love. He wanted to see her, and he went and saw how beautiful, but cold and pale she now lay, in her beautiful casket, surrounded by flowers, his beloved (I would rather say: his "sacrifice").

After walking back home from the church, Mr. Ford had complained to his daughter that he was not feeling too well. The daughter was frightened and at once she rang their family doctor, and her sister who was not at home just then. They both arrived within a couple of hours, only to witness his life's thread break before the dawning of the new day.

With the mail, Erik brought happy news. Ever since my arrival in this country, I had been

227

corresponding with my school friend Ellen. I had not heard from her for a while, but now a letter had arrived. She was in this country now, and she was going to come and visit us very soon. She wrote that seeing as how I had named her a godmother to our son, of course she must come and see him. Now I lived in happy anticipation, I would have cheerful company, as Ellen was going to stay with us for a couple of weeks.

We had finished the hay making, and Erik returned to the logging camp for a while. Then I had to run some errands. I forget what. I brought the children out in the yard to play and told them not to go in. There was an old carriage by the house, and I put some hay and a large blanket in the carriage, and told the children to climb in there, if they got tired. Little Erik had done that several times before. I left for the errand, listening to the children's merry laughter on my way. I began to feel unhappy; why did I have to go and leave the poor little ones alone, even if it was for a very short time and it was a beautiful day and they promised to be good. I even tried to sing:

Jos ruikutella voisin

mä kielin sataisin

ja leivosena voisin
kohota pilvihin.

If only I could croon
in a thousand tongues
and as a lark soar up to the clouds.

But singing did not comfort me, and I was ever so happy when I got to start back home so soon that

228

the children would never guess that I was already on my way back. I was not all that far away from home when an animal stood up right next to the path. I thought it was a wolf and was frightened, but as it began to move, I realized it was only a deer which fled into the bush with its white tail waving in the air. Then I reached the gate, but I could not hear the children's voices though by now I should have been able to hear them. I ran to the carriage, and little Erik lifted his head, frightened and said: "A bear came into the yard." I did not believe a word. I just thought that the children had been frightened, and they had begun to imagine things, because they were alone. The whole bear story was forgotten.

Erik was at home again. He went out and brought the cows home. One night he came in looking so worried that I asked him, has something happened? He said that our black cow was lying on the ground, badly torn, with a bears' pawprints all around her. He said he met a neighbor that said that a bear had taken a calf right out of their cowshed. The door of the cowshed had been left open for the night, and the bear had ripped the boards apart.

One day, I had just finished washing up after the midday meal, and I sat down for a moment. Again I began to wonder when Ellen would arrive, or would she manage to come at all this summer. But when she does come, we shall certainly reminisce our school days, the times when we were still free from all the life's worries. I was brought out from my thoughts all of a sudden, at the sound of a knock on the door. I went to open the door, and got a great surprise. Standing there, extending a hand to greet me with a handshake was Teuto Ikola. He said: "Truly, Anni, you did go and get married, didn't you, and you did not wait for me, even though my mother asked you to wait. Did you believe I'd never grow up to be a man?"

"Well, you sure did grow up, and a handsome man you've become, too," I said, "but how is your mother?" Teuto said his mother was outside waiting. They had not been quite sure whether they had come to the right house, so she had told Teuto to come and see, while she waited. I asked Teuto to sit down and then I rushed to ask Mrs. Ikola to come in. And so began a long chat. We had to talk about everything that had happened since we last met. I remembered all the good advice Mrs. Ikola had given me. I asked about her daughters and the well-being of their family in general. Then the talk turned to the Ford family, and I asked how my former employer, Mrs. Ford, was doing. Mrs. Ikola said that Mrs. Ford was living her life exactly as she had before her husband's death. For her, her sense of duty was her first and last priority, as she did her bit for the society, working at the post office. She never gave any cause to gossip, and she never spoke of her life. She really was a paragon of tolerance, I thought. To have her husband stolen in such a way should have made her take a very open stand in the earliest stages of the whole affair.

Then Mrs. Ikola reminisced about Vilho Niemelä's visit to the town and their home. She described how Vilho had stood there looking at my wedding picture, so deep in thought that it had made Mrs.Ikola conclude that "Vilho would have been the right man for you dear Anni". That made me laugh, and I told her that Vilho had also dropped by at our homestead. He too is married now, I said. The Ikolas left, and I remained sitting there for quite a while, deep in my thoughts. How the words of even a good friend can lead one badly astray.

I thought about the past, trying to grasp elusive images. Finally I came out of these thoughts, as if awaking from a dream. Was this me, I whose motto had always been: "Everyone is the master of their own life?" Was this me, giving free rein to the images wandering around in my brain? Certainly not! Did not Mother always say when I was little: "What goes around comes around"?

Why, I had been finding fault in everything, even become resentful towards life and my surroundings. I had forgotten this golden rule: to make the world a better place, one must start with oneself.

Could I believe at all, that everyone had a "destiny"? Was not our life exactly what we made of it? Was I, who had always been happy, about to sink into depression? No, no, it must not happen. Just take it briskly now, face life straight on, with open eyes, and sing like the sailor boy:

Hurraa me nuoret meripojat!	Hooray, we young sailor boys!
Ilo onpi meillä aina,	We are always cheerful,
eikä meitä surut paina.	sorrows cannot bring us down.

(To be continued)

Episode 42, 7 Dec 1954

Then my long-awaited visitor arrived. Oh, Ellen! I did not know how to best welcome her. It was so good to see her. Her first words to me were: "Had I seen you, Anni, in some theater, up on a stage, in a big role, I would not have been surprised in the least. But to see you here, deep in remote wilderness, as a pioneer's wife and a mother, I am truly amazed. I would not have believed that this life would suit your cheerful character at all. Why, even at school, you would take the lead in everything, and perform the hardest roles in every dramatic play. Can this all be real?" "Everything is just as you see it," I replied, almost adding: this is my "destiny", but then I remembered that I did not believe in such things.

Erik came in. I introduced him to Ellen, and they greeted each other as if they were old acquaintances. Erik said that he knew Ellen already, because Anni had spoken of her so often. After Ellen had had a meal and some rest, we went out to see the vegetable patch. Ellen said suddenly: "When I saw your husband, I don't know why, but a poem we read in school came into my mind, do you remember this one?"

On aate pyhä ja kallis

Holy and precious is the cause

jonka puolesta taistellaan.

for which we are fighting.

Jos Herra voiton meil' sallis,

Should the Lord grant us victory,

ois onni se Suomen maan.

all Finland would benefit.

"I remember," I said, "but now you must tell me everything that has happened in your life since we parted at school."

Ellen said she was afraid that not that many interesting things worth recounting had happened in her life, except when she had been working as a guard in a women's prison. She had gotten this job when her father died. Ellen's father had worked as a guard in the Hämeenlinna women's prison for several years. When Ellen was only two years old her mother died, but Ellen had the kindest stepmother. Ellen told me how this good mother always had a tasty snack for her, when she came home tired from the prison, and how she, returning the favor, would pick up some of her young stepsister or brother's socks or pants that needed repairing. But slowly everything began to change. When she came home in the evening, she had neither appetite nor a friendly word in response to her mother's greeting, she just wanted to go to her room and cry, cry right from the bottom of her heart.

I asked: "Why"? The women prisoners had become acquainted with their warm hearted guard, and they had begun to tell Ellen their sad life stories. One woman had been betrayed by the man she loved blindly, and she had murdered him. Another woman's beloved had been faithless, and she had killed his mistress. A young girl had told Ellen about her shame, she had killed her baby. Another young girl had killed her suspicious father in order to save her mother, and so on. They told Ellen so many sad stories which they had never told to her father. In Ellen, the women had found a compassionate listener. This went on for some time. Then Ellen realized that this work, dear though it was as she had inherited it from her father, was too hard for her health. She decided to quit the job, and leave for this golden land in the West.

In the first night, we were out in the yard, sitting on the grass. Our youngest child looked tired. Ellen picked up the child in her arms. We began to sing:

Oi muistatko vielä sen virren,	Oh, do you still remember that psalm
jota lapsena laulettiin?	we used to sing when we were children?
Kun yö yli akkunan yltyi,	When the night crept across the window,
se virsi, se viihdytti niin.	that psalm, it gave such comfort.
Se virsi loi rintahan rauhaa,	That psalm soothed troubled hearts,
se uskoa unehen loi.	in dreams, it brought faith.
Oi muistatko vielä sen virren,	Oh, do you still remember that psalm,
niin laula, nyt laula se, oi.	if you do, please, sing it now, do.

Ellen enjoyed herself so much, wandering around in the beautiful woods. She would be gone for hours on end, and sometimes I was afraid she had gotten lost. One day, I was in the yard, listening hard

234

in case Ellen had gotten lost and was shouting for help, but there was no shouting to be heard. Instead, I heard singing and then the words:

Mun armaani	My sweetheart
ei lemmi tummaa	does not love dark-haired girls
Hän lempii vain vaaleata.	He only loves the fair-haired girl.

Oh, I see, I thought, she must be in love, but I did not have the heart to tease her when she came into view. A couple of weeks went by in this cheerful fashion. Ellen's opinions on my life had changed, and one day she exclaimed, thrilled: "I almost envy you. You can live so freely here, in the beautiful nature. Not even the best career as an actress could compare with the life here, in the wonderful nature."

She always returned from her long walks brimming with delight. One day she came in, out of breath, but her eyes shining with joy, and she told me that she had seen a beautiful doe with her fawn.

One day at mealtime, I was again waiting for her to return from her walk. I was getting tired of waiting, and the food was getting cold, so I went out to the yard to call her. And there she was, on her way back, singing a mournful song, of which I heard these verses:

Mä orpo olin nyt,	I was an orphan now,
kaikilta hyljätty.	deserted by everyone.
Voi miksi en mä silloin	Oh, why couldn't

voinut kuolla.   I just
                                         die back then?

I would accompany her on her walks whenever I could find a moment between my housekeeping chores. This time we decided to go down to the lake, but first Ellen wanted to go and see the small field where the summer rye that Erik had been talking about was growing. He had told Ellen about it. It was the product of Erik's hard work and efforts.

When we arrived at the edge of the little field, Ellen exclaimed, excited, that she had never seen such beautiful, tall rye. I said, it grows well here, but it does not grow this tall in Finland. Then I recalled the only rye field that I ever saw in Finland. I asked Ellen, did she remember that preacher man, Lindgren, who lived next door to them, on the outskirts of the town. Ellen said she did, and asked: "Why would you ask about him?" I said that this Lindgren had a rye field. My Mother used to go to this preacher man's meetings, she was a devout listener. When the preacher man's rye crop was ripe for harvesting, Mother went to help pick the ripe seed heads, and she took me along. Mother spent a whole day picking the seed heads, working hard, and I tried to help as best I could. When the owner had all his crop harvested and ground to flour, he did not even give my poor Mother such flour as would have been enough for porridge, to thank her for her hard work. Though I was so little, I could see that my Mother's feelings were badly hurt. Mother could not hide her disappointment well enough from me, and I accidentally overheard her mention something about it to Father.

236

My story did not surprise Ellen all that much. She just said that she remembered many more stories of Lindgren's stingy ways, having lived next door. Then we went down to the lake, and Ellen began to sing:

Kun mä kuljin pitkin	As I was walking along
Näsijärven rantaa,	the shores of the Lake Näsijärvi,
ystävääni kaipaillen.	longing for my friend.
Niin ne aallot,	The waves
jotka suutelivat santaa,	that were kissing the sands
kertoi ettei hän ole tääll'.	told me he was not there.

(To be continued)

Episode 43, 10 Dec 1954

The lads next door had learned that we had a young lady visiting us. They began to make up all sorts of errands and whatnot to have an excuse to drop by. Ellen, possessing such a sweet disposition, was always friendly to them and found something to talk about. But one of our neighbors, a bachelor called Jukka, had not heard that we had a visitor, so he dropped by, on some errand of his, wearing his everyday work clothes, and his pants had a big hole in one knee. When I saw Jukka in the yard, I went to the door and asked him in for a cup of coffee. He came in, and Ellen was at home, so I introduced them. At once, Ellen began to chatter in her friendly fashion, but Jukka grew more nervous by the minute. Sitting on a chair, he covered the hole in his pants knee with one palm, but with Ellen chatting so enthusiastically, poor Jukka forgot the hole completely, removed his hand, and set his foot on the floor. Then he remembered it again, and with a loud slap he hastily put his hand back over the hole. Finally he grew so agitated that without saying a word, he left and went to sit on a bench in the yard, but Ellen followed him and kept on chattering away as if she had not noticed anything special.

Finally Jukka left, and we were splitting our sides laughing, while Ellen was wondering why on earth that poor man was so upset. She did not understand why we were laughing until we explained the cause of our merriment to her. Ellen thought it was perfectly natural that on a workday one would dress accordingly. She had not realized that Jukka was flustered because a city girl saw him in such ragged clothing. Jukka dropped by again on the following day, but now he was wearing such Sunday clothes that we thought he was on his way to town.

On Sunday, after the morning chores, we took the children along and went to call on a neighbor who lived some distance away. We had to pass that little cabin where we lived in that first summer while Erik was building the house on our homestead land. Ellen wanted to stop there for a little while, and I told her how one day, when Erik was away from home, a terrible thunderstorm broke out and fierce winds began to blow. I was very frightened, and I nailed blankets to the windows to shut out the brightest flashes of lightning. Outside, the loudest crashing was going on, as trees were falling down criss cross around

238

the cabin. I expected a falling tree to smash the roof at any moment, and I was sitting on the floor, scared, holding little Erik in my arms. That night in that horrible weather, Erik came home, soaking wet, afraid that something had happened to us.

"Look," I said to Ellen, "the trees are still lying there, some big ones right next to the cabin, yet none of them managed to hit the roof." "It was providence," said Ellen. We had been living in the cabin for a few days, when I saw a snake on the floor. Right away I grabbed up the baby from the floor, climbed on the bed and began to scream. Erik ran in and asked: 'What's the matter?' I stuttered something and pointed under the bed. Erik saw the snake, ran out and got a hay fork. He killed the snake, but more and more kept coming out from under the bed. Erik killed them all and then counted them. There were sixteen snakes. The floor boards were few and far between in that particular spot, under the bed, but still we could not figure out how come the snakes had nested there and could not find another way out. I even pitied them, because there are no poisonous snakes around here, but nevertheless it felt creepy to have them so near. Erik killed them all, he showed them no mercy. Then I showed Ellen some holes in the hillside. Many of them housed lots of round eggs which were soft, and not hard like bird eggs. Erik said they were turtle eggs. There were always plenty of them on that hill, because the ground was so sandy, and maybe that is why the snakes liked it there, too. On our homestead, we had heavy black soil, and we never saw any snakes or turtles there.

Then we walked the rest of the way to the neighbor's place. We had such a good time in their company. We sang old folksongs, such as this one:

Suloisessa Suomessamme	In our sweet Finland,
oisko maata armaampaa	there cannot be a more precious province
kuin on kaunis Karjalamme,	than our beautiful Karelia,
lauluin kuulu kotimaa.	land famous for her songs.

The neighbor's wife asked if we knew the song about the mountainous lands of Tyrol. Ellen and I said almost as with one voice that we sure did, and so we sang:

Tyrolin kauniissa vuorimaassa	In the beautiful mountains of Tyrol
se vaunu kiiruhti kulkuaan.	a carriage rolled on hastily on its way
Siin' istui vaunussa kalvas sulho	In the carriage sat the pale-faced groom
verevä morsian rinnallaan.	with his blossoming bride by his side.
Mutt' kolmanten' oli kuolema.	But the third one riding was Death.

Then she asked us to sing the song called "The

convent bells", and this is its first verse:

Ja lumi se peitti maan avaran	and snow covered the wide open land,
ja luostarin kuorissa veisatahan	and they are singing in the convent.
Kuule: luostarin kellot ne soivat.	Hear: the convent bells are tolling.
Ja ritari kannettiin taistelusta,	And a Knight was carried from the battle,
hän haavoissaan oli niin kalpeana.	wounded, he lay, so pale.
Kuule: luostarin kellot ne soivat,	Hear: the convent bells are tolling,
ne soivat, ne soivat.	they are tolling, they are tolling.

Yes, they carried the Knight over to the convent, to be nursed by a nun. The poor nun fell in love with her patient who was healed, then rode off. The last verse of the song used to bring tears in my eyes when I was little. This is how it goes:

Hän riemulla riensi pois	At dawn he rushed off,
etelähän,	to the south
Mutt' nunna jäi kammioon	But the nun stayed in the chamber,

itkemähän.	weeping.
Ovat luostarin ruusut oivat,	The roses of the convent grow beautiful
mutt' nunna ne viimeiset	but the nun took the last roses
seppeleks' loi	and created a wreath
ja riemuisen morsion päähän	for a happy bride to wear on her head
ne toi.	she brought them.
Kuule, luostarin kellot ne soivat,	Hear: the convent bells are tolling,
ne soivat, ne soivat.	they are tolling, they are tolling.

It was time for us to leave, to be home on time for our evening chores, but just before we left, rain began to pour down in heavy torrents. Then the husband promised to take the children and Erik home first, and bring back raincoats for Ellen and me. We got the raincoats, but the rain seemed to fall ever harder. I was sure that after this experience, Ellen would no longer consider my life so delightfully romantic, but I was wrong. She even liked the rainstorm. Had we known the song "Pennies from Heaven" back then, Ellen would certainly have sung it. However, we did remember one song about rain, here's the first verse:

Jo sataa, sataa, katsokaa,	It's raining now,

242

nyt kasviraukat juoda saa.	raining, look now the poor plants have water to drink
Ne päänsä nostaa jällehen	They lift their heads up again
ja kumartavat riemuiten.	then bow down joyfully.

We walked along the narrow path, with difficulty, in silence, and great raindrops kept falling down our necks from the drooping branches of the large deciduous trees. We were both deep in thought.

I would have liked to know Ellen's thoughts, for surely it was now if ever, that she would lose all her admiration for my life and see it only as my monotonous "destiny". I was deeply worried that a fragile girl such as Ellen who was not weather-hardened like me, would surely catch a cold after this freezing bath. I wanted to strike up a conversation with Ellen so that I could put my worries aside. Finally I said: "I'm getting frightfully hungry". Ellen said she was, too, but her voice sounded somehow hopeless, and it was easy for me to imagine what she must be thinking. I was sure that she was saying to herself, that we would go on being hungry, seeing as here we were, the cooks, padding down a winding, slippery path, in torrential rain.

(To be continued)

Episode 44, 14 Dec 1954

At last we made it home. Erik met us at the

door, to help us take off our dripping wet overcoats. Ellen was the first to enter the room where warm, sweet smells of food greeted us, and Ellen exclaimed: "Oh but it smells wonderful in here, we are absolutely starving." Erik rushed to us and handed Ellen a steaming cup, saying: "Ladies, please wait a moment before eating, first you better drink up a hefty dose of hot infusion, against colds, then change into dry clothes, and then sit down for supper. The infusion will warm up your insides, and the hot stove will do the same to the outsides, my good ladies."

Ellen obeyed. She took a deep sip, made some faces and hiccuped. Then we sat down for supper. Before taking her seat, Ellen went to have a quick look at the children who were sleeping quite peacefully. Erik said he had fed them as soon as they had gotten home and put them to bed right after the meal. Rainy weather makes children dozy, and grown-ups, too, said Erik. Having finished his meal, he got up from the table and said to me in passing: "Now you two keep each other company, I'll do the evening milking by myself tonight." Ellen said she was feeling very well now, and she was wondering how thoughtful Erik was, having known to prepare for us some medicine against colds, and an even bigger wonder was that he had fixed such a good meal.

Ellen did not realize that in the wilderness one learned to put food in store for times of need, so anyone with the slightest inkling of the noble art of cooking was able to whip up a meal fit for a king by opening a few tins and jars. I just said that Erik had had to learn to cook while I was in childbed, and not just that, he had had to develop good nursing and child caring skills, but he vows that next time he'll be

244

sure to take me to the hospital. Actually, we have had a kitchen helper when necessary, but all nursing and child care has been left in Erik's hands.

The rain had ceased during the night, and in the morning the weather was bright and beautiful. Ellen took off for her customary walk. When she returned, she had her arms full of all sorts of branches from deciduous trees. She decorated the whole room with them, so it looked more like a leafy garden pavilion than a house, and she was so delighted, like a child with a new toy.

Our evenings passed quickly, as Ellen had brought some good books. There was: Kotkat" (The Eagles) by Hilja Haahti, the well-known writer, along with others. We took turns reading them out loud, after we had managed to put the children to bed.

Sometimes the talk turned to our birth country, and it turned out that Ellen knew a bit of Hilda and her mother. Then Erik interrupted us and said that he had not remembered to tell us what he had learned on his last trip to town. He had heard that Hilda was in the very last stages of consumption, and that her mother was extremely mean to her. Doctors had ordered Hilda to drink rich milk, but her mother said that skimmed milk was plenty good enough for someone who was no good for work. I wanted so much to go and see Hilda, and tell her that Toivo had never left her, instead she had been the victim of her mean mother. But I had to wonder whether that knowledge would have given Hilda any consolation in her last moments, or just caused bitterness towards her mother. It is hard to say. After this story, we felt so sad that this song came into mind:

Elämä katoo kuin unelma vaan	Life fades away as if it were but a dream
ja vuodet ne vierivät pois.	and years, they slip away.
Aika se virtana pois kiirehtää	Time goes by like a rolling stream
niinkun se varjo vain ois.	as if it were but a shadow

Soon Ellen's summer vacation was drawing to end, and we were yet to visit my Father and his wife at their homestead. We decided to pay them a visit. It was amazing that my Father recognized Ellen and remembered her surname, though he did not remember her first name.

He was in high old spirits, and he recalled plenty of amusing stories from the times when Ellen and I still went to school together. Then he began to tease Ellen, asking how come she had not yet found herself a man. Ellen assured him that she was sure to get around to it eventually, having first roamed around this great western land a bit. But the fact that Ellen talked so much about returning to Finland made me think that she must have a sweetheart there.

My Father's wife did not chatter much, but then again, she had plenty to do. Their youngest child was the same age as our youngest; a little girl called Esther. She did not walk yet, she just sat, contented, in the middle of the floor. She sure was an exceptionally beautiful child, with big blue eyes and cheeks of pretty red porcelain, and she did not even shy away from us at all. Then we said good-bye, and as we were walking homeward, Ellen was wondering about

246

how my Father had changed. Entirely gone was the posture of a Finnish gentleman, and he had lost a lot of weight, only his voice and manner of speech were still the same, Ellen said.

Having made several promises to visit us again at our homestead and to write soon, Ellen went back to town. As she was taking her leave of us, she said she was so happy to have had this opportunity to live right here in nature. And that she had learned many interesting and useful things about nature. She said that for her, our simple and healthy way of life would be a cherished memory, compared to life in town. Wistful, I watched Ellen go, believing we would surely meet again one day.

Soon after Ellen's departure, Erik wanted to go to town and buy a horse. There was not much money, but he said he would make a down payment, and take out a mortgage for the rest. He went to town and came home with a handsome horse, but it was an arduous trip, some forty miles of walking.

It was a miracle how much he was able to achieve with that single horse. Logs for the sauna were hauled in, new fields got made, and of course a stable for the horse got built. But then we fell behind in the monthly payments because Erik was not working outside the home. The Jew came to repossess the horse, but he did not settle for just the horse, he took everything we had mortgaged: the harness, the cart, and the only milking cow we had at that moment. He took everything to town, planning to hold an auction, but he did not get any buyers because people had heard that those possessions had been robbed from us. A relative of ours had opened a store in the town, and when he heard about the auction, he went and bid on the cow at the bottom price set by the Jude, 28 dollars. No-one else would bid, so he got the cow. At once, he sent word to us that we could come and collect the cow. We never found out what happened to the rest of our belongings. And it was only a few times that we had had to go to our neighbor's for milk.

I was feeling so bad that I could not sleep for many nights, and I could not understand whether the law allowed repossession of all mortgaged items even though the Jude got his own back, plus all the money Erik had already paid.

(To be continued)

Episode 45, 24 Dec 1954

But Erik never gave up. He went back to the logging camp, and I spent all my evenings making handicrafts.

Then a team of land surveyors arrived to our area, and they wanted Erik to work with them. Once the lines had been run, great machines were brought in to dig ditches in the marshes. They said that the dirt they dug up would be laid on one side of the ditch, for the construction of roads. Erik said that as soon as the ditches are dug, he will bid for a road construction contract and buy a team of horses to get the work done. I tried to stop him, but he said: "If you do nothing, you get nothing."

And of course he was right. When he brought the great horses to our gate, little Eric was at the window, full of anticipation. He ran out, absolutely thrilled. Then he came in, out of breath, and said:

248

"Father says that Mom should come out and take a look at the handsome sight." I said to him, "Go tell your Father that Mom is not excited". Choking back tears, the lad ran out to his father and repeated my words to him.

For sure, they were good horses, but I was afraid of debt, while Erik was not. He got the road construction contract and all sorts of haulage contracts, and he was always working.

Then we had a new neighbor. One day, Mr. and Mrs. Leppi came knocking on our door. When I went to open the door, I almost did not believe my eyes. Standing there were Erik's good old friends from town, the couple to whom Erik had taken me when I was being made a bride. At once this poem came into my mind:

Mua morsioksi sitten laitettihin	Then I was being made a bride
Hän kukkasetkin mulle sitoi päähän	I was crowned with flowers
Ja toivon onnen rintahani jäävän.	I wish happiness lives in me forever

To Erik, the arrival of the new settlers was a great pleasure, and a great benefit, too, for now he had a partner for hunting and work.

And I was ever so glad to have Mrs. Leppi drop by every now and then. After all, several weeks might still go by without me seeing a single outsider. Late one afternoon, I saw a group of men crossing the marsh, walking towards our house. When they came closer, I saw that they were Indians, each carrying a

249

heavy pack on his back and a gun. I hoped that they would pass us by, but no. They dropped their heavy loads and guns in the yard and came inside, without knocking. There were five men, and the children were afraid of them and climbed up on the bed to sit there. I was very much afraid, too, but I tried to put on a brave face. The men said they wanted food and coffee, and hastily I began to set the table, thinking to myself, I bet if Erik were at home now, they would not dare boss me around like this. They got a big meal and they kept asking for refills of coffee. When they were finally leaving, I was sure that they would give me some meat, in payment for their meals, but no, they just hoisted up their packs on their backs, and left. They must have set up a camp somewhere nearby, because a few days later an Indian wife came to borrow some bread, and she promised to bring some meat as soon as they had some. I gave her a loaf, and a couple of days later she was back, to borrow another loaf of bread, with the same promise. She came a third time, too. Then I said, I have no more bread for you. She said, "Give me some flour, then." I gave her some, but she never came back and we never got any meat. We had no more visits from the Indians. Perhaps they had moved their camp further away.

On several occasions, I had to go after the cows again and leave the children alone at home. Once, I left them on the floor and told them to be good. When I hurried back and ran inside, I looked around the room, scared. It was absolutely quiet in the house. I went to the bed, and there they were, poor little babies, sleeping with their heads together, with fresh tears still on their cheeks. Seeing them almost made me cry, and I had to wonder how they had managed to get on the bed. The next day, the mystery was solved. I went out and left the children in the house. I came back quietly and, unseen, to find out what they were doing. The youngest one did not walk yet, but was able to stand using a chair or bed for support. As I was watching and listening, I heard Little Erik say to his younger sibling: "Grab hold of the side of the bed." Then he lifted her by the legs, telling her to hold on tight. In this way the child managed to clamber up on the bed, and Little Erik climbed up after her.

But when I came home on another day, I found them sitting on the floor, next to the box stove, and they had an empty matchbox on one side and a big pile of used matches on the other side. As soon as I got over my astonishment, I asked little Erik what he was doing. He said he would strike one match at a time. Then Maria put it out at once and placed it in the pile which grew ever larger as the matchbox got emptier.

Surely a guardian angel had been watching over them, so they had not set fire to their clothes, and I could not scold them, but after this incident I hid the matches so well that never again did they wind up in the children's hands.

Shortly before we got the horses, Erik said, this year we won't be turning the soil with spades, rather he'll go and ask Mäkelä to come over with his team of horses and plow the potato field for us, and in payment, he will go and work for Mäkelä. I was so happy, now our potato field would be done much more easily. Two years back, we had sown our former potato field with clover seed, and now it was growing so pretty and sweet-smelling. But when Mäkelä came over, he said that all big farmers make their potato fields from clover fields, and he began to plow the clover field.

When I saw that, I burst into wild tears and said to Erik: "Please don't let him plow the clover field, it's the product of our hard work, and we just cleared new land for potato." But Erik said nothing to the plowman, he just consoled me: "One day we'll have our own team of horses, and then we can plow wherever we like."

Our land was flat, and wet in rainy times, but when Erik got the horses, he plowed the land and made strip fields just as they were made in Finland. He measured the width of the strips carefully, and dug deep ditches between them, to prevent rain from making the strips waterlogged.

I have talked about neighbors, and by then there were actually quite a few families living in the wilds, but several miles apart from each other, so that by modern standards, we had no neighbors at all. Yet one morning, I woke up early, I could hear a strange cowbell clanging somewhere near. Erik was not at home, he was on a two-day trip.

I got up quickly, still groggy from sleep, threw on some clothes and ran out. There were strange cattle in our grain field, the fence was broken. I grabbed whatever stick I found and ran as fast as I could to drive them away. But I had been in such a hurry that I had run out barefoot, and I happened to tread on a board with nails sticking out of it. One nail sank deep into the sole of my foot, and I could not pull it out until I sat down and yanked hard. Then I went back to driving the cattle, I chased them away and mended the fence. I had no time to think about my injured foot. I even did my morning chores and fed the children, but then the foot began to swell up, and it was aching horribly. Deep desperation gripped me.

(To be continued)

Episode 46, 28 Dec 1954

Deep desperation gripped me. I was sure I would die from blood poisoning, after horrible pains. What will happen to our poor little children then? And Erik was not coming home until the next day. There was no help, no recourse, no way whatsoever to bring in a doctor. The children saw my agony, and they were ever so quiet. Then we heard movement outside. Erik stepped in. He walked to me, and with great effort I managed to ask: "How did you come back now, I already lost all hope, I was sure that only death can end my misery." Erik said he had slept very little last night. He had had a nightmare which had made him feel that something had happened at home, and he had left for home as soon as the day dawned. He put some hot poultice on my foot, fed the children and saw to them. Then he tended to the cattle. Then he went to town for some medicine for my foot. The foot was still throbbing painfully, but now at least there was hope for life. Erik returned amazingly soon, completely exhausted, of course. He brought a jar of tar, opened it and began to boil up some. When the tar had boiled enough to thicken, he laid a fat warm layer on a piece of cloth and wrapped the cloth around my foot. The pain stopped, the swelling began to go down, and soon I was able to walk.

Then two world-famous events occurred. We saw Halley's Comet. I cannot remember for sure whether it was in 1911 or 1912. And then there was the shipwreck of the Titanic. It was in all the newspapers, and they even wrote a song about it, but I do not recall it just now.

Then we were expecting a new heir, and Erik found out which hospital I could go to, which doctor would be attending to me, and when the doctor said I should leave for the hospital.

Erik had begun to build an extension to the room. But that work progressed slowly, because one of the neighbors asked Erik to help out with their building work. I was growing ever more nervous day by day, and I tried to ask Erik to do only our building work, but he said he would have the room done well in time for the arrival of the new baby.

That year, I had chickens, and they were laying so well that I was able to send eggs to town quite often. One night Erik said that next morning, he would go to town. That night, I put the eggs in the crate and the cream in the jug so they would be ready in the morning. In the morning, I got up quietly, went to the stable and fed the horses, then I made some coffee and went to wake up Erik, saying: "All's done, hurry up now, off you go." Erik began to get up, but he was so slow that I got annoyed and said: "Come on, hurry up, I've given you a hand, you don't even have to feed the horses."

Erik said that he had had a dream that he won't be going to town that day. Now I got mad and said: "Don't you dare turn lazy on me. Last night you said that you would go, you and your dreams." Then I

254

remembered how Erik had had a dream when I injured my foot and had come home though he was supposed to be away for one more day.

That moment, my anger evaporated, but for another reason. I felt sick. That night a little baby boy was born. In the morning, Erik ran to our nearest neighbor to ask him to go ask my Father to get us a nurse. The nurse would not have found our homestead if my Father had not acted as a guide.

The winter was beautiful and spring seemed to arrive soon now that Erik was spending his nights at home. By day, he hauled lumber with his team of horses to the side of the railway line. Then the summer came, and an especially good year for berries. On his hunting trips, Erik had found good berry patches beyond the marsh. He said that in town he had met a man who wanted to buy blueberries, and promised to pay $4.00 a bushel.

Erik said: "Let's go out to the berry patch and make it a picnic. Anni, you fix enough food for the whole day, I'll take the kids there and then come back for buckets and pails, so we can pick plenty." When we got there, the fields were all blue with big berries.

The children were seated on blankets, and they were so happy there, that Erik and I managed to pick plenty of berries. I tended to criticize Erik's picking, for being so dirty, but he always had more than I did.

When we made it back home that night, exhausted, Erik did most of the evening chores, saying he reckoned I better start cleaning the berries, so he can take them to town in the morning. I spent all night cleaning the berries, but I was ever so happy to have plenty, in several paper boxes. Early in the morning,

Erik headed to town with the berries, and I was trying to calculate how much we could get for them. When the clattering of the carriage began to sound, I went out in anticipation, but as soon as Erik drove into the yard, I could see that the berry boxes were still in the carriage. I turned white in the face and stuttered, why, didn't they want the berries? And I gave Erik a searching look, but his face did not seem the least bit worried. He said: "These berries were far too pretty. They're shipping berries out of state, so half the load must be leaves and raw berries. Anni, you start washing up jars, I'll get the big pots and start cooking jam. We will can it all and have enough berries for the whole year." We set to work, and we worked through the night. We put all the berries in two-quart jars, and got some two hundred quarts of rich jam.

In the morning, we went out picking again, and soon all boxes and pails were brimming with berries. Erik was having fun, saying it was his sort of picking, not having to worry about leaves and whatnot, but, typical of me, my berries always tended to be too clean. I recall that we spent several days picking berries, as we were able to sell them fast, and we had all we needed for own use already canned up.

It was a good year for cranberries, too. Mäkelä came over carrying a large grain sack, and he handed me a bundle. He said it was salt pork, and he asked me to make him a 'mojakka' with it, as he was going to go pick cranberries from our marsh. He picked for a couple of days, filling up his sack, but I did not cook that pork mojakka just for him. I prepared versatile meals for my family and invited Mäkelä to join us at the table.

But I was wondering to myself, that man is so

thoughtless, picking his berries almost in my yard, so I must go further away to get berries for us. But I did not run out of tricks. I took a sharp ax and cut down the alders which had been growing at the edge of the marsh and hiding it from view. Once I had felled the alders near the house, I was able to go cranberry picking and still see the yard. I seated the children in the old carriage and told them to stay and play there, forbidding them to go into the house. In that way, the children were able to see me and they were happy. After several days of picking, I had filled up a fifteen gallon barrel. I topped it with water and covered it with a lid and a weight, and it kept well for a long time in the outdoor cellar.

(To be continued)

Episode 47, 31 Dec 1954

In the following summer, two large ditch digging machines were brought into the wilds. Huge ditches were dug, and the dirt was spread on one side of the ditch as a road. In our lake, the water level sank so much that the shores became dangerous for the cattle, until they learned to stay away. Many cows fell in the lake, but Erik managed to haul them out somehow. Still, one young bull did die, only its head remained visible. Erik had come too late to its rescue. Then one of the horses fell in, but, as if by a miracle, Leppi, along with a friend, happened to drop by just then, and together with Erik, they rescued the horse from certain death. We shall always remember it with gratitude. They sure were friends in need.

A couple of years passed. We heard from Ellen

every now and then. Her sister, along with her husband, had arrived from the old country, and they settled in a big town in Ohio. Ellen moved there, too, and she got a good job with the family of a millionaire. Ellen wrote that her sister gave birth to one son after another and soon they had three sons. We had so much fun when she wrote and told us their names: the first born was Panu Pekka Kalevi, then Juha Jaakko Tapani, and the youngest, Asla Aimo Sakari. We thought the names did not sound so good here in America.

Then Ellen wanted to have pictures of our children, but of course we did not even have a camera. From old habit, I decided to try my hand at drawing, and on a piece of paper, I drew a picture of each child, one next to the other, trying to show how each was taller than the other, or the other way round. When I sent the picture to Ellen, she made out to praise it, saying I did not need a camera, and that she could easily recognize Little Erik in that picture. However, I could not help thinking that the drawing was a pretty poor effort and lacking in many respects.

Ellen said that she was very comfortable in her job, but as a poor Finnish girl she was finding their wasteful ways simply awful. She was a housemaid, and one day, when the mistress once again told her to take a load of clothes to the trash, just because they were no longer in style or their son had grown out of them, Ellen asked, could she not take them and send them to a friend living at a homestead in Minnesota. The lady of the house told Ellen to take whatever she wanted. So Ellen was able to send us plenty of good clothes. When I altered them for the children, and even for myself, we were always well

258

dressed. The clothes which arrived for Little Erik needed no alteration. The millionaire's son was a little older so when he outgrew his clothes, they were exactly the right size for Little Erik.

Our neighbors had several school-aged children, but there was no school. As the distance to the school in the town was too long and too difficult for the transportation of the children, the town school board visited us, too, to see when our children would become school-aged. Some two miles away from our homestead towards the town, a large shack made of iron sheets was standing empty. It had been used as lodging for lumberjacks. The school officials turned it into a classroom, but it was difficult to find a teacher who would accept a job in the wilderness, as there was no house nearby where a schoolmistress could have boarded. Finally they found a man teacher. He settled for living in the classroom, where one corner was set apart as his bedroom by means of curtains. At first, only four children attended the school. After three months the teacher got fed up and he left. In the following winter, the school board made another attempt at finding a teacher. They found a man who had been working as a land surveyor. He was used to walking, so he accepted the job. He lived by the railroad, but outside town, so he was able to leave his wife for a week at a time, and hike through the wilderness, carrying a backpack, to teach at our "school". He was excellent at everything. He even tried to farm some land, and once he asked Erik if he could plow him some land with a one-horse-plow. Erik agreed to go, and off he went, with the teacher and our gelding, some eight miles across the wilderness. As they were leaving, the weather was beautiful, but it turned cold soon, though it was May.

As Erik was leaving, I said to him: "I'm anxious about staying here alone with the kids for so many days. Suppose the mare decides to foal while you're gone." He just laughed and said: "Don't you worry, Anni. Nothing's going to happen, and I'll be back in two or three days."

I went about my chores, and the day passed quickly, but as night fell, I grew very frightened. I used to sing to the children every night when Erik was not at home, but that night I could not have felt less like singing. The children began to ask, Mother, aren't you going to sing to us tonight. I consoled them, "I will sing to you again tomorrow night, I'm just so tired right now". The children were a bit unhappy, but soon they fell asleep anyway.

I slipped out, to try and see if I could hear where the mare was walking. Upon leaving, Erik had put the mare in a small pen so that she could walk right up to the wall of the house. The night was pitch black and very chilly. It had begun to drizzle, or sleet, really. As I was standing there, shivering, maybe with cold, or maybe with fear, I heard movement right next to the wall. I ran inside, got a flash light and went out again. When I pointed the light towards the sound I had heard, I saw, to my horror, that it was the mare lying there on the ground. I was sure she was thrashing and kicking about in her death throes. I went back inside, but I could not even think about going to bed.

I made several more trips to check on the poor mare, assuming she had died. Obviously she had gotten up on her feet, because she was in a different place. But again she was lying flat on the ground. She was breathing in great ragged gasps. I did not dare go out again. Instead I wrapped myself in a blanket, shivering terribly. Eventually, I fell asleep, all worn out, and I woke up at first light. My first thought was, Erik will be so sorry when he comes home and learns that the mare died. I dressed up quickly and went out. The rain had stopped. Though I did not want to, I could not help glancing in the direction where I saw the mare lying on the ground last night, but she was not there. Now this amazed me. I thought, suppose she got better and she is up on her feet. I walked to the opposite end of the pen, alternating between fear and hope, and I was shaking so hard that I almost tripped over my own feet. And there she was, standing in the corner. Upon seeing me, she wheeled around quite showily. By her side there was a handsome foal, standing on somewhat wobbly legs. After all the fear and excitement, my nerves grew all numb, and I burst crying, even though I should have been laughing because the mare was not dead after all.

Then it began to sleet again, and the foal seemed to be shivering. I began to lure the mare into the stable. I opened the gate and the door to the stable, but the mare, having first followed me a bit, turned back because the foal was not coming. I got some grain in a bucket and let the mare have a taste. She followed me a little further, and this time the foal was coming, too. It took quite some time and effort, but finally I got the mare and foal into the stable.

(To be continued)

Episode 48, 4 Jan 1955

I set the grain bucket on the floor so the mare could have her fill, but I did not dare walk past her and go out through the door, instead I went to the window, removed it with great difficulty, set it down on the ground outside, gently so as not to break it, then I climbed out of the window, and ran quickly to close the stable door, before the mare gobbled up all the grain and came back out. When I had the prop pressing against the door, I had won, and I heaved a sigh of relief. Then I went and got some hay and water and gave them to the mare through the window. She accepted everything I offered. I brought her some more grain three times a day, a little at a time. But each time I had to use a different old bucket or pail, because while the mare was eating, she managed to move it out of my reach as I fed her through the window. The mare must have wondered why I did not come in through the door, but I did not dare, in case she tried to come out when I opened the door. The foal had warmed up in the stable, and was gamboling around happily.

When Erik came home a couple of days later, the children rushed to tell him: "We have a baby horse." Then I told Erik about my first night's fears and terrors, expecting him to say: "Oh, you silly little girl". But he did not say so, even if he might well have thought so. He just said: "Well, Little Mom, you sure had to a lot of trouble, and you sure took really good care of the mare." He did not even scold me, when he found several buckets and pails stuck in horse manure as he went to let the mare and foal out.

He had already unharnessed the gelding, and the gelding was standing free near the stable door, waiting for his companion, whinnying now and then.

But when the mare saw the gelding, she was no longer as friendly as before. When the gelding approached, the mare immediately positioned herself between her foal and the gelding, so that the foal could not follow the gelding. However, these bad manners did not last long, and the gelding won the foal's friendship completely. It was amazing to see how the foal, right after nursing, ran to the gelding, and together they galloped to the woods, at high speed. The mare would stay behind, grazing lazily in one spot. At first, she used to whinny after the other horses, but later she paid them no attention whatsoever. The gelding, a somewhat flegmatic sort, had grown younger, and he frolicked around just like the foal

Finally arrived the memorable day when Erik was able to leave to collect the full homestead ownership documents, for we had "proved up" our claim by living on our homestead for five years and farming it as set out in the law. At the same time, he would also become a naturalized citizen of America. He had to go to town and then take a train to the city, and as this was not an errand one could complete within a single day, once again he had to spend the night away from home.

In those days, there were bears about again, and Erik had set a bear trap on a path some distance away from the house. In the morning, as he was leaving, he remembered the trap and said: "Now I have no more time to go and spring it, and I forgot it last night. Anni, you take that path tomorrow, walk some ways in that direction, and listen for any rattling of chains. If you hear anything, don't go any further, but come back home as fast as possible." I promised to follow his orders to the letter.

The day passed easily, for there was always plenty to do, and now we also had four children. They were a lot of work, although they were good kids. At first nightfall felt dreary because Erik was not at home, but I began to tell to the children that tomorrow when Daddy returns, we shall all be full naturalized citizens of America. They asked, what does it mean, and I tried to explain as best I could.

As usual, I sang old Finnish folksongs to the children. Soon they were in dreamland, but I just could not manage to sleep. Among other things, I kept wondering to myself, suppose there's a bear in the trap when I go and check it tomorrow, but then, Erik did tell me not to go too close. I did fall sleep eventually, and when I woke up, I clearly remembered the dream I had. We had received a letter from "Uncle Sam", and when we read it, it said: "Because you, Erik Ahola, and your family, have proved up your homestead in such an excellent fashion, "Uncle Sam" will hereby grant you a reward, a great big Holstein cow. You can pick her up in town." That was all I could remember.

The children waited for Daddy just as eagerly as I did. It was 22 October 1913. When Erik arrived, quite late in the afternoon, he brought presents for the children. They were ever so quiet, and I asked Erik about each and every detail of his trip. He said that getting the homestead ownership papers took only a few minutes, but the naturalization papers had taken longer, because there were half a dozen applicants, and each applicant was asked several questions, especially about the US system of government, but the same questions were not asked from all

264

applicants. Luckily, Erik was not the first to be tested, so while he was listening in on the others, he tried to recall answers to all the questions for which he had studied the "Nilsen and Lundeberg Almanac" so hard. When his turn came, he answered all questions on the system of government correctly. Then followed a long string of personal questions, and everything went well until the judge asked about the birthdates of our children. The first was born on the 10th of the month, the second on the 9th, and when Erik said that the third was born on the 9th, the judge corrected him, you already said the second child was born on the 9th of the month. Erik had said that his second, third and also the fourth child were all born on the 9th. The judge had burst into good-humored laughter, and said: "Well, Erik, then your first child should have hurried up a bit, and not linger until the 10th, so all your children would have been born on the 9th day". Then the judge clapped Erik on the shoulder, shook his hand, and welcomed him as a naturalized citizen to the great nation of America.

When he finished recounting all the stages of his trip, he asked: "Did you remember to check the bear trap?" I said I had checked, and that I had thought I heard something, but was not entirely sure. Then I told him about my curious dream. All he said was: "Anni dear, maybe you were a bit wound up, so you had a weird dream." He changed into work clothes and said he'd better go and check the trap right away.

When he returned, he whispered in my ear so that the children did not hear: "There's a big deer in the trap. Maybe that is the cow "Uncle Sam" promised, that you saw in your dream."

(To be continued)

Episode 49, 7 Jan 1955

The digging of the huge ditches had been completed. The big "house boat" which traveled in the water in the ditch behind the machines, had already been taken apart and moved away, but the digging machines were still there, surely waiting for orders for transportation to another site in another locality. Some contractors had viewed the dirt banks, bidding on the contracts for leveling the dirt into roads. The new roads did not benefit us all that much, because we had to clear about one mile of road by ourselves to reach the dirt bank road, and we also had to build a bridge. At that end, they offered Erik a contract, too, however not for the road towards town, but towards the Leppi farm. He decided to accept the offer, as we had a strong team of horses, so work would go fast. Little Erik said he would go to the road site with Daddy and make him coffee, seeing as how he was now six years old, and his father promised to take him along.

Everything seemed to be going so well. Erik was pleased, reckoning he was going to earn reasonably good money in that job, and Little Erik was enjoying himself, eating Mom's tasty lunches at the site and playing on the dirt banks to his heart's content. Erik praised that the lad was good at making coffee in a tin pot over a campfire.

However one day, Little Erik ran home, screaming miserably: "Mom, Mom, I burned my face." I looked at the boy, in absolute horror. His face was red and completely covered with coffee grounds.

266

Now I had to act, and fast. I took some lamp oil and kept pouring it over his face until all coffee grounds washed off. Then I settled him on his back, got some thick cream and gently applied it to his whole face. While the cream remained cold, his face did not burn, but as soon as the cream grew warmer, the pain returned. His face swelled up, his eyes closed, and he could open his mouth only a little so that I could feed him with the tip of a spoon. Erik had not been able to leave the horses and come home with the boy, but he arrived soon afterward with them. When he came in, he asked at once what I had done so far. When I explained, Erik said that rinsing with lamp oil had been a good measure, but unless we bandaged the lad's face, he would have scars for sure.

Erik took a wide pan, put some deer fat in it to melt, and he told me to tear up plenty of cheese cloth into strips about two inches wide. He soaked them through in the liquid fat. Then he proceeded to bandage the boy's face with them. Even his eyes were covered, and a narrow gap was left only for the nose and mouth. The lad said that the pain had stopped, and soon he fell asleep.

Then Erik told me how the accident had happened. The boy had put the lid on the pot so the coffee would boil faster. He was lifting the pot off the fire with a stick when the coffee began to boil. Steam blew the lid off and the coffee into the boy's face. Indeed, it was a lot of work, worrying and nursing, changing the bandages. But then the result sure was nothing if not a miracle. Not even the tiniest scar remained on Little Erik's face.

Erik got us a little dog. The children named him "Prince", but Erik laid down a strict law, nobody was allowed to play with the little dog. Erik began to train him to herd the cows, and he was such a quick learner that soon I had it much easier with the cows. He learned each cow's name, and finally nobody had to go and bring the cows home, they came home all by themselves. When Prince saw the cows coming, he stationed himself near the barn door, and there he stayed until each animal stood in her own stall. If one of the cows went into a wrong stall, Prince would go and nip her lightly in the leg, and at once she would go into her own stall. Then Prince would wait by the door for me to come and tie them up. He never left his station, though I did not always make it to the barn the moment the cows came in.

Then we began letting the cows out to stretch their legs every day in the winter, too. When I let them out, they would first gallop at full speed to the pasture. After a while they returned, walking in a line, led by the bell cow. They came straight to the well, where I was already pumping water into the basins. The bell cow always drank her fill first, and then the others, in their turn. Every now and then they shot a glance at Prince who was standing there, stock-still, poised to nip at any cow who tried to jump the queue without waiting for her turn. When the last animal had had her drink, Prince fell in line behind her and stopped at the barn door. It is hard to believe that an ordinary dog could ever become so smart. Many a visitor thought he was simply amazing.

Once, two cousins of mine came for a visit. One of them had recently arrived from the American front in France where he had spent thirteen months, during World War I. The stories of his experiences made for especially interesting listening. Then I said that I had to

268

go and let the cows out to drink. The lads said: "Now, Anni, for a change, you stay inside, and we'll pump the water and let the cows out." I thanked them for their kindness, and the lads left to do the chore. I watched through the window how they filled up the basins. As they let the cows out, at once the cows jogged off to the pasture. The lads came inside, upset, and they said: "The cows got scared of us and they ran into the woods, now how on earth can we get them to come back home?" "Don't you worry," I said, "they will come home, and then Prince will see to them. When they return, you can pump up more water as they drink it, and then they will go into the barn in good order." "Well, if that was not the most peculiar thing we ever saw," the lads said when they came back in.

Then the members of the school board paid us a new visit, to see how many pupils they could expect. Little Erik was now in school age, but it was simply impossible to send him off alone for a two-mile walk in deep snow, in cold weather. At the time, Erik was hauling lumber to town, past the school, and the school board proposed that Erik give the boy a lift to school, and then pick him up on his way back home. That is how Little Erik got his start at schooling, but it did not add up to a full term, as lumber was not being hauled every day. Then the teacher proposed that the school be open only in good weather. The school board agreed and promised to pay us fifty cents a day for transporting the children to school. Now Maria was also school age. We took the children to school in the morning and picked them up at night. Soon Prince figured out what was happening. He ran to the school with the children and then he came home. At night,

Prince sat by the door, tilting his head to the side, and when I was leaving to pick up the children, he was already far ahead. The children used to say, Mom does not have to take us to school or back home, Prince will take care of us.

(To be continued)

Episode 50, 11 Jan 1955

One night, the teacher came to see us again. He walked with the children, with Prince happily romping around them, running ahead, and then falling behind. After a chat on this and that and the other thing, the teacher asked, would we consider swapping a milking cow for a large, pregnant one. Erik reckoned, sure, but how could they be transported? The teacher said, seeing as the weather was so dry, he could walk the cow from our farm across the wilderness, if we let Little Erik accompany them, so the cow might go more willingly. I had doubts, would a little boy manage such a long walk, but the teacher had it all planned already. He said that they would take their time and make it a slow hike. On the next day, he would put the lad on the train (they lived right next to a train stop) and Little Erik could ride by train to our town, where his Dad could pick him up and give him a lift home, as Erik was due to go to town on that day anyway. When Little Erik heard this discussion, nothing could have kept him from going, especially because he was promised a train ride. So it was settled, and everything went well. Little Erik would not even admit to being tired from the long walk. All he would talk about was the fun of the train ride. The teacher brought the large, black Holstein cow over to our farm by himself. She walked behind the teacher like a dog, she did not even need a rope. She had always been pampered but here she ended up in different circumstances.

The teacher led her to an empty stall, and at once she settled down. The teacher sat on her back, and one corner of a handkerchief was peeking out of his pocket. The cow pulled the handkerchief out with her teeth, and she probably knew other tricks, too. The teacher spoke to her as if she was human, but from the very beginning she was in Prince's black books. When she was let out with the other cows and she failed to come back with them, she had Prince nipping at her heels in no time. It was not a good idea to mention that cow's name (it was Biuti) when Prince was within hearing range, as it would really make him all worked up and send him chasing her. When the cow had had her calf two months later, the teacher came over again. He said: "I will milk Biuti and your other cows tonight." Reckon he also wanted to fuss over Biuti while he was there.

The years of World War I then arrived. One after another, friends and relatives were drafted and sent across the ocean to fight for freedom and democracy. Sugar rationing was in use, but we were not affected in any way. Rationing was based on headcount, and by then we had several children. Besides, the children were used to wholesome and versatile food with less sugar. Then a strict flour rationing system was put in place. Though wheat flour rations were small, along with other types of flour, again we did not go short. We had good crops of wheat and rye in our own fields. At first we did our threshing in the way it was done back in Finland. When farmers living a couple of miles away got harvesting machines, we began to take all of our grain there for threshing. It was a lot of work and we had to leave all the straw there as we could not bring it home for our own use. During that war, all good citizens had to buy Liberty Bonds in order to cover the government's war expenses. We also had to buy Liberty Bells, or Piggy Banks, for the children. The keys to the Piggy Banks had to be left at local banks. In this way, many children saved their few pennies because of the war.

One Saturday, Mr. Leppi came to call with his wife. We always had such a good time when they dropped by. In a previous chapter I have recounted that they used to live in town and we stayed with them when we got married. Now that they were our neighbors, they seemed almost relatives. Mr. Leppi came in, took his wife by the hand, and said to me: "Listen, Anni, I usually "beat" my missus at home, but now I thought, if I gave her "a beating" here, that ought to fix her good and proper!" (Editors note: Finns are known to swat themselves with birch branches in the sauna to increase the blood circulation near the skin). For a moment I could not figure out what he meant, but then it dawned on me, and I burst out laughing and told him that Erik was already out at the sauna house, taking firewood and water there.

Mr. Leppi went out to see Erik, and Mrs. Leppi began to speak, saying that actually, there was something they wanted to talk about. She looked at me, and I blushed. Then she said that she and her husband had decided that, seeing as how we were again expecting a new heir, and Erik had told them that he was going to take me to the hospital well in time, they would love to have our youngest child in the meanwhile. Erik would manage with the older children. I was ever so touched by the kindness of these good people and I said: "Surely it is far too much trouble, for you have not had a little one in years. "It is precisely why we would love to have her," Mrs. Leppi said, "we both love small children." And so it was settled.

I got a letter from Ellen. She said that she had joined a young ladies' sewing club. They met once a week at someone's home. They had knitted and sewn plenty of clothes for needy families, and children's clothes were their special favorites. Ellen had told them about us, and the young ladies had become all excited about sewing and putting together a veritable stork shower for me, to be delivered by mail. Actually, they could not just mail the parcel, for its contents had grown so numerous and diverse. It arrived by Express baggage. Ellen said that they had really enjoyed themselves putting it together. Even for each of the older children there was something, a pair of socks or mittens, or a shirt. I thought that this saying in the Bible certainly applied to them well: "It is more blessed to give than to receive."

I was away from home for over three weeks, and of course Mr. and Mrs. Leppi came soon to see me, and to wish the baby well. Mr. Leppi carried our little Margi into the room. The moment she saw me, she ran to me quickly, climbed onto my lap and grabbed me around the neck so fiercely that I felt fit to choke, and it was almost impossible to hold back my tears. Soon she climbed down, then she picked up her hat and coat, took them to Mrs. Leppi and said to her: "Auntie, let's go now." With this, little Margi brought tears to both our eyes. Margi wanted to go back with them, so they had to slip out unseen by her.

A few weeks later, Margi had forgotten that she had been the Leppis' little darling. They came to visit, and Mrs. Leppi told me a secret: now they were expecting their very own little Margi. I congratulated them and said: "No wonder, seeing as you had such a good 'model' for almost four weeks."

Mrs. Leppi was an unusual neighbor in that she never gossiped. If I told her something I had just heard, she would say that she had heard it long ago. None of us could possibly foresee that that treacherous enemy, death, was stalking the whole family. First, the oldest daughter fell sick, then the oldest son, then Mrs. Leppi herself. Their little Margi, as the Leppi couple had christened her, was healthy and beautiful. But then their youngest son fell sick, too, yet none of their condition seemed serious at the time, we all thought it might be just a cough.

Time went by again, and we reached the fall of 1918. It was the driest fall we could remember in this state. A hard, driving wind blew every day, even the watery marshes were drying up, and clouds of smoke began to appear here and there at the fringes of the marshes. Then stories of forest fires began to circulate, yet everyone was still hoping for the arrival of the reviving rain. However the rain did not come, instead drought became ever more menacing. Smoke clouds covered the sky and the wind blew day and night. At night, we could see flames riding the winds, yet they still seemed far away. We were beginning to run short of flour. Erik decided to take a load of grain to the mill for grinding. I got up early in the morning to

274

ready him for the trip, as by horse and cart the trip to the mill and back home would take nearly a whole day. The weather seemed a bit clearer, and the wind had calmed down.

(To be continued)

Episode 51, 14 Jan 1955

The children and I stayed at home. We had all kinds of chores to do. Even as Erik was leaving, he warned us not to light a fire in the stove, in case the wind suddenly picked up again. In the afternoon, a strong wind did begin to blow again, all of a sudden, and the sky was covered by such thick smoke that we no longer saw the sun. From the windward side, burned leaves began to fly into the yard. We rushed to pump water and fill up all buckets, pails and barrels. I set ladders against the walls and helped the older children to climb up onto the roofs and haystacks, and then I hauled up a bucket of water to each. I soaked all possible sacks and large pieces of cloth in water, and we wrapped them across our shoulders and on top of the haystacks so we could put out any burning branches and firebrands that flew up there.

We kept a draconian eye on everything, so fire could not break out anywhere. My heart beating in agony, I waited for Erik, afraid that on his way home he might get caught amidst those horrible flames, but I did not dare put my fears to words. Finally, a terrible fear came over the children, too. They wanted to climb down, and they wailed at me: "Mom, Mom, where can we go?" I tried to comfort them and I said:

"If everything catches fire, we will run into the lake, we will have enough time for that, but let's wait a little and see if Dad's coming home." Then we heard the clattering of the cart, and we ran to the gate to meet him. When he jumped down, we saw that his clothes had burn holes in many places. In addition, the mane of one of the horses was burned, as was a part of the cart. He told us that as soon as he had unloaded the grain, he hurried home. He would not stay and wait for the grinding. He had seen that the wind had turned to the direction that was dangerous for us. In one place he had had to drive the horses at a gallop through the flames. That was when the cart had caught fire. However, he always had a bucket for watering the horses on the road, and with the bucket he got water from the ditch, put out the fire in his clothes and the cart, and rinsed the horses which were on the brink of exhaustion.

Erik was ever so pleased that we had been so alert and made sure that sparks had not yet managed to start any fires in the yard. He said: "The horses can rest now, in harness, while we take turns pumping water, and fill up all the barrels that the ditch diggers left." We did not feel hunger or exhaustion, because we were battling for our very survival, for our lives, and for the safety of our children. There were no fires yet near the Leppi house, so Mr. Leppi came over with a couple of men. The horses were put in front of a rock sled. The sled was loaded with full water barrels, and hauled over to the windward side, where others, armed with wet sacks, were beating out flames coming in over the ground. At night, the blaze grew a little smaller, but one could not trust it, it might flare up again at any moment. And we had to stay up for several nights in a row putting out fires, when the wind suddenly changed direction. With great effort, we managed to keep the house and yard from burning down, but all haystacks that were further away did burn, as did tall stacks of lumber. The children said: "Now all the lumber for our new room is gone." I consoled them and told them to be grateful that all our lives had been spared. Just a couple of miles south of our farm, a whole family had burned to death, only the father survived, as he had not been at home. The blaze was at its most terrible on 12 October 1918. When the wind finally died down and rain clouds appeared in the sky, many people were grateful, even though the area looked so desolate, and the peat bogs were still smoldering here and there. One rain made the world safe again, but it did not snow until the first of November and I was happy when that snow hid the whole tragedy under its white blanket. After the fire everything looked so sad and desolate. Here and there, peat bogs kept smoldering until late autumn when the first snow hid the grim blackness under its white blanket.

Erik had to take me for another "stork run", but when we arrived in town, the doctor had sent us a telegram: "Do not come to hospital under any circumstances, burn victims and dying everywhere." He told me to stay in town, at a nurse's home, and he promised to come and see me as soon as I sent word that I needed him. So I stayed in town, waiting, and Erik went home very downhearted. Several times, my nurse tried to get in touch with the doctor, but every time she was told that he was out, seeing a burn victim somewhere. Finally she got some good man to go and fetch the doctor. In fact he brought two doctors, but by then I was already at death's doorstep, and did not even know what had happened. I only knew that I had to return home from my "stork run" with my arms empty. I was still young, and my health appeared to be mending. Erik had come to see me the very next morning.

Of course, the fire was the culprit for what had happened to me, because I had had to struggle so hard. And they also blamed it on the fire that a terrible influenza began to rage. When Erik brought me home, everyone there was well, but perhaps I brought the germ with me from town, because at once the children fell sick, and I ended up completely bedridden again. Little Erik was ten years old, and he was the first to fall sick, but he got better in a couple of days. Then he was the only one in the house who was able move about, and he tried to see to the cattle as best he could. Too much hard work and struggle must have weakened Erik so much that the flu hit him hard. One of our neighbors had let the town know of our state, and from the town, the Red Cross sent us food and plenty of bread. The doctor came by, too, and left us medicine. Back in town, he had then wondered whether any one of us might survive. I suppose it was the Finnish sisu, but Erik got well within a week, as did the children, only I remained seriously ill. I could not sleep at all, and after ten days of sleeplessness, I was afraid it had affected my sanity. The moment I closed my eyes, I heard noises like gunshots, or someone climbing in through the window to kill me, and I tried to get out of the bed to escape my enemies, but I did not have the strength to get up. Then I saw a man by my bedside; I began to scream for help, I screamed: "Erik, Erik, come help me." He was standing right next to me, but I did not see him until he said: "Anni, calm down! This man is the doctor, and he wants to help you." Erik's voice always calmed me down, even when I was in the throes of real nightmares. The doctor gave me a shot in the arm, but even that did not help me sleep. However the pills he told us to dissolve in hot milk began to soothe my nerves little by little, so finally I could sleep a little at a time, but my eyes were sore and swollen from much waking.

The Ikolas had moved away, and I heard that Hilda had died. She had left a little boy, born four months after Hilda's arrival in this country. Now Hilda's mother had the boy whose father and brother were in Finland, maybe even unaware of Hilda's sad fate. I had thought that it would be nice to go and see poor Hilda, but now it was too late. She had moved to the mansions of Tuoni and left her little boy in the care of a mean grandmother.

A terrible epidemic of influenza began to rage everywhere. In our household I was the first victim, but when they were taking me to the hospital, I was glad that nature was covered in layers of beautiful snow. The disease struck everyone, some harder, others milder, but even the sickest patients felt their hearts vibrate and swell with joy on 11 November 1918 as peace was declared and the world war ended. Everyone talked about permanent peace and the peace conference initiated by President Wilson.

(To be continued)

Episode 52, 18 Jan 1955

After the doctor left, the word about my uncertain condition traveled to the neighbors. My Father also heard the news. At once, he came to see us, no longer an arrogant overlord, rather a broken man. He took a seat at my bedside and began to talk. He said that he had been so very wrong when he had tried to separate Erik and me, and were his good wife not so hard set against his actions, he would have made good on his threats. Then he said that he had caused us so much trouble and hurt. Finally, he could not speak any more. Instead he burst into uncontrollable tears. I never saw a man cry so. Great big teardrops were actually falling on the floor. Then he begged for forgiveness, first to Erik, then to me. Erik was instantly willing to forgive and forget. But it was different for me; I promised to forgive, but I did not say whether I could forget. When he was at the door, on his way out, I overheard him saying to Erik: "This must be the last time I will see Anni, she cannot possibly recover, that is what the doctor says, too," he concluded.

During his brief illness Erik lost almost all his thick brown hair. But he regained his health, and he got us a housemaid so that he could go to work, hauling lumber to the railroad. Every night, he would first come to my bedside and ask: "How is Little Mom now?" When the same question repeated night after night, and I was not getting any better, it finally began to get on my nerves, and I said to Erik: "Stop asking how I am doing, you will certainly see if I begin to get better, or else I'll die."

After that, he would just holler at me from the door: "Hello, Little Mom." One day, I finally felt that I had grown a bit stronger, and I sat up. I asked the girl to give me clothes and a comb, but I could not properly manage to comb my hair, or get dressed, so the girl helped. Our housemaid had fixed supper, and I asked her to set a plate for me, too. Then we waited for Erik to come home. When he looked into my room and saw me sitting, dressed and groomed, he did not say hello or ask how I was, instead he wordlessly grabbed me in his arms and carried me to the table, to my own place, with tears from his eyes rolling down my neck. The children were delighted and they said: "Now Mom is going to get better!" The meal started, however I could not swallow a single morsel. I felt the blood drain from my face. I touched my face. My face was cold and I was passing out. Erik saw it, and quickly he picked me up and carried me back to bed. After supper, the girl came to help me undress.

Then our excellent school teacher came to tell us that he was not able to continue teaching, because of the difficult trip between home and school. His wife needed him at home. He said that the school board had already arranged for our children to go to a boarding house in town. Erik would have to take them to town, but the board would not pay for their transportation home for weekends, instead they paid for full board for the whole term. So the children were taken to the school in town, where all teaching materials were of course much better than in our little school.

Finally my health was restored and I could run the household by myself. At first I was anxious whether the children had enough clean clothes to wear at school, because after the lumber haulage was finished, Erik went to town only once a month. After visiting the boarding house, Erik said that the children had a wonderful matron. Each day, she laid out the children's clothes, and she always had the dirty clothes packed up for Erik to take home. In fact, the biggest credit belonged to Ellen. She kept sending so much clothing that it was easy for me to keep the children clean at school. But it sure made a mountain of washing once a month, and the ironing was downright exhausting.

Several times Erik and I thought about moving away from our homestead, to such a location that the children could go to school from home. Erik had been looking here and there, but all populated places were expensive, and another new beginning in untamed wilderness seemed daunting, not because we still did not have youthful energy, but because we now had a large family. Once, I sank into veritable desperation, and sat down to write about my worries. Actually, this happened before my illness and two years before the fire, in 1916. I sent my effort to a Finnish-American periodical, and I received a response from a kindhearted lady who consoled me in my times of trial, and later I would occasionally receive such uplifting letters from her that I felt I no longer bore my "fate" alone. I had the best friend in the whole world, only a pen friend, yet of such great importance to me. During my illness, I had received many comforting letters from her, and now I wrote to her that for the sake of our children, we had to move away from this "Paradise of Eden".

Between his other jobs, Erik had been building a room from large logs. The walls were already at roof level, but that is where the work had halted when all our lumber burned in the great fire. Erik was wondering, what on earth were we to do with that incomplete room, if we moved away. Now we had a fifth child starting school in town. Erik occasionally brought the children home from school for the weekend. Almost every time the Fords' son, who was only six months younger than Little Erik, came along with the children. He fitted in with our crowd so well that if he did not come, we missed him. Previously, I recounted his birth when we were still living closer to town and his father's death when he was not yet five years old. The lad took to calling Erik "Dad", just like our own children, and in the lad's mind, the name stuck to Erik for his whole life. Whenever he saw Erik, he called out from afar: "Hello, Daddie Ahola!"

But now I'll resume the story of our moving plans. Erik found an 80-acre parcel of land right next to a road, with a small school some half a mile away. A river teeming with fish ran through the property. I wanted to go and see the property, but we had three little ones at home, and I could not leave them anywhere. I had to rely on Erik's good judgment. He made the down payment on the parcel of land. Then he bought boards and tar paper, and took off to build a cabin on the new land. One day, when he was home, I said to him, we must go and say good-bye to the Leppi family. It was so sad to leave the neighbors who were so dear to us. Mrs. Leppi came some of the way to see us off, and there, in the heart of the wilderness we said our good-byes, with tears streaming down both our faces. I could not possibly foresee that it would be the last time I saw Mrs. Leppi.

Erik had finished building the cabin on our new land. Little Erik came home from school to help with the move, and the cart was loaded full up. I sat on the bench, Little Erik was driving, the youngest child was riding in my lap, and two little ones were sitting on a mattress behind me. The trip seemed ever so long. In reality, according to the survey lines, we traveled only four miles to the west, but the winding road more than doubled the distance. Finally we turned off the road and pulled up in front of a tar-paper cabin. Erik came out, and he said: "Oh, Little Mom, it is so good here. Climb down now, the world's best fish mojakka is stewing on the rocks. This morning I caught a big fish in the river, and I cooked it especially for you."

"Oh my goodness, it is so bleak here. All those big trees so near and all their branches burned off." "Never you mind, Little Mom, we'll soon build us a home, and we'll replace those trees with beautiful fruit trees," he said.

Erik had prepared a great surprise for me. He had gone and asked some of the neighbors to come with their horses and haul the logs of the unfinished room from our homestead. We could already see one log load after another turn off the road towards our new land. Erik hurried off to point where each load should go. All the logs had been marked so that he could easily set them back in their correct places. He said that the neighbors had promised to come out again to help put in the windows, doors, and the roofing. He even had all the shingles done, so we would be able to move in in the fall. It was in 1921.

Now this is all I am going to tell you, little ones, because your bigger sisters and brothers can tell you what happened then. You never saw our old homestead, because you were born when we already lived here. "Oh, Mom," said the youngest of the Ahola children, Elizabeth, Jaakko and Antti, almost in unison, as Anni Ahola finished her story. "But

284

we would still like to know one more thing, what happened to Ellen and the Leppi family?" said Elizabeth.

"Well, Ellen's sister moved back to Finland with her family, and Ellen went with them, it was some time before we moved here. Ellen died in Finland in 1923 at the age of 34 years. As for the Leppi family, their oldest daughter died first, then Mrs. Leppi in 1921, then their oldest son. Their youngest son spent several years at a sanatorium for consumption patients and they discharged him to die at home, but his good father nursed him at home for another five years before he died. And the youngest daughter Margi was completely spared from the grip of that dreadful disease.

T h e   E n d

Appendix A

The Translator's Notes:

Serendipity: A wonderful word coined by Horace Walpole in 1754, describing the faculty, fact or instance of making fortunate discoveries unexpectedly, by accident. It is the perfect description of this fascinating project that has brought closer together not only generations, but family members as well. Renewed family ties, new friendships – all products of a wonderful stroke of serendipity.

My involvement in this project is just one example of serendipity among numerous others. I discovered that some great-great-uncles and aunts had emigrated to the United States in the late 1800s and early 1900s. I wanted to learn what became of their lives. However I felt reluctant to pay membership fees for genealogical internet databases for uncertain results. I hatched a plan to recruit a paid-up member to do some data lookups, in exchange for whatever help I might be able to provide here in Finland.

And so, on the Finlander Forum there is David, looking for a Finnish-to-English translator. He had received a series of stories authored by his Grandmother. However, the stories were in Finnish. Now a translator was required so that non-Finnish-speaking family members, David himself included, could read them. Nothing ventured, nothing gained, I wrote David proposing a trade: translation for data lookups.

Cautiously, David agreed to a test run. He sent out the first batch of stories. As soon as I read the first couple of paragraphs, Amalia held me firmly spellbound and I was keen to start.

During the course of this project, I felt serendipity at work on several occasions. Among the most fascinating discoveries were that there both Amalia and William turned out to have geographical connections to me. Amalia was born in Jokela, Tuusula, and my family and I live in Järvenpää, only some 15 kilometres away. William was born in Alavieska, northern Ostrobothnia, province of Oulu, only some 50 km away from my hometown, Oulainen. Some of my roots go back in time to Alavieska, so a family connection is also entirely possible. Both these geographical links meant that I had knowledge of places and local dialects, which came in handy for deciphering some expressions and references Amalia used in her stories.

Translating Amalia's stories was engrossing and enlightening. This is how I first described Amalia's stories to David, before beginning the actual translation work:

I took a quick peek at your Grandmother's stories, and they make lovely reading. She was a good writer, she had the ability to bring the people and places to life — I can well visualize the events and the conversations in my mind's eye. She depicts real life, close up. It was not necessarily all that straightforward to translate in places, where cultural aspects may most likely require some explaining. But so far it seems

b

very workable. Except for the songs and poems — I'm not going to try and make them rhyme in English, as I'm pretty useless at rhyming even in Finnish ;-D I'll just translate the contents, and you can then tackle the rhymes, if that's OK by you :-D

And this is how David responded to the first two story translations:

I received the first of the stories and I am in shock as to how close to her life these stories were. I wait with baited breath to see the next one!

My reply summarizes the translation strategy I adopted for this project:

Yes, the stories really do bring people and places to life, don't they? They really do make interesting reading. Amalia had a good eye for detail and excellent memory to match. Amalia's writing and word choices reflect their time very well. Sentence structures seem pretty idiosyncratic to her, so in most cases I've translated them as they are, splitting long sentences into shorter ones only occasionally.

I've flagged obvious typos and added notes where I feel they might be necessary, but I won't be going into grammatical explanations, as I'm sure that the grammatical rules were different back then. So, for example, I won't be pointing out where two or three separately written words should actually be written together because they make up compound words — it might not have been the case back in Amalia's time.

I could have made the translations read more fluently like idiomatic English, but I feel it would detract from Amalia's personal style, and of the general flavor of older times her writing conveys. That's why I've chosen a fairly straightforward translation style, smoothing out or rearranging translated sentences only where the result would otherwise be overly awkward for no good reason.

You'll also understand now what my reference to numerous poems and songs meant — Amalia's averaging a good two or three poems or songs per story, and they all rhyme. What amazing memory she had for songs and poems. In that she reminds me of my own Grandma, who sadly passed away in 2005, at the age of 96 years. I swear she remembered every song, poem, riddle and story she ever learned. — Now I digressed. What I meant to say is that if you like, I'll keep pointing out the songs, hymns, etc. when I recognize them, and will tell you which ones are still around.

Music certainly featured high among the many aspects I enjoyed during the course of this project. It was wonderful to encounter so many songs learned in childhood, or otherwise. All this familiar and cherished music seemed another instance of serendipity, another link between author and translator.

More serendipity came in the form of David's discovery of an earlier set of Amalia's stories, published in Päivälehti in the 1940s, a decade earlier than the Keskilännen Sanomat serial. These stories

d

added material and insight. It was interesting to compare the two sets, to see whether or not things were included or how they had changed, if at all.

All in all, this project went quite smoothly. The only major snags we hit that still remain unresolved are a couple of expressions no-one has been able to decipher. They may be very local Finglish, or may have been introduced by the typesetters as unintentional but utterly misleading typos. They take nothing away from the stories or their readers, though they will keep on nagging at their translator for a long while. Goodness, but I'd love to find out what on earth that "kuutti" is!

David, thank you so much for entrusting me with your Grandmother's stories. I feel awed and delighted that you welcomed me to participate in this project that has helped bring generations and family members closer together. David and Margaret, thank you for the greatest stroke of serendipity: the gift of your friendship. My family and I will always treasure it.

Päivi Torkki translated this Finnish written anthology. Päivi was educated at the University in Turku Finland, and holds a MA in Translation and Interpretation Studies, majoring in English. The University of Turku has always had a strong, internationally known position as a multidisciplinary scientific university. The Turku academy was founded in 1640 and is thus linked to the family of universities of the continent.

Among her places of work besides Finland, she has practiced her art in Singapore and Australia. These stories have retained the flavor as well as the structure of the original writing due to special efforts made by Päivi. Along with the straight forward hard work of the translating, she spent time reading the rest of the newspapers. This included the local news of surrounding communities and even the advertisements. Although curiosity was no doubt a factor, this additional research rewarded her with an appreciation of the Minnesota temporal and vernacular Finnish, isolated from Mother Finland. It also made it possible to understand some of the unique colloquial uses and phraseology.

Music is an integral strand throughout the work. Päivi too has this great love of music. She sings in Järvenpään Naislaulajat Ainottaret and regularly performs with a quartet for fun but also in competitions. She has a great husband, Asko, and three great precocious children, daughters Aliisa and Sini, and son Iikka. The family has two Australian Terriers. They live in Järvenpää, north of Helsinki.

f

Appendix B

A tribute by A.W. Havela, President of Keskilännen Sanomat.

This was published on 7 February 1955. It appears here in its translated form.

Various creatures living on this earth have given rise to various metaphors. Even such a small critter as the ant has come into the attention of man long ago, along with its great industry. We have learned that there are different kinds of ants, hard working and idle. The busy worker ants are always on their feet, making sure that their sweet home is not allowed to fall into ruin, rather its roof rises higher and higher every day. The idle ants only want comfort. They are like parasites. They do not care how each day passes and turns to night as long as there is even a little bit to eat and some corner where they can while away the daytime. Recently my thoughts latched onto the above mentioned metaphor as I was reading the long-running serial "Elämän Ulapalla" that has been published in this newspaper and that has now been announced to have reached its conclusion. Under the title appeared a modest pen name "Anni Ahola", whom I have since learned to know as Mrs. Wm. Kytölä, presently of Wright, Minnesota. Every now and then I read locality news columns penned by Mrs. Kytölä, but little did I know that the name also belonged to one of our American Finnish folk writers who wrote such a long and successful epic for our periodical.

In this story, many American Finns have been able to recognise their lives as if portrayed on stage, though they themselves have lacked the creative writing skills that Mrs.Kytölä possesses in such obvious abundance. Like Runeberg, I pondered how a writer puts ideas into words:

Ne korutont' on kertomaa	They tell a plain and simple tale,
ne ota, kallis synnyinmaa.	accept them, oh precious land of birth.

(This is a quote from "Second Lieutenant Ståhl's stories by J. L. Runeberg)

With plain and simple words, Mrs. Kytölä has related a great part of her life in "Elämän Ulapalla", yet many other characters have also been brought in as "guest stars", giving this pleasant series even more substance and style, which in turn made its plotting so elevating that with great anticipation the reader has looked forward to the publication of the next issue of this newspaper, to be able to read the next episode of this sympathetic story.

Some learned and highly educated people have always been able to write thought-inspiring observations of life, but considering that now we are focusing on a person whose education was limited to a few years of elementary schooling, it becomes an entirely different matter.

h

The author of "Elämän Ulapalla" is just a single industrious individual who has worked hard to advance her life since a very young age. She is the worker ant to which I referred above, one who never feared work. Together, she and her husband made their first home in the wilderness, far away from other people, with only deer and bears as occasional visitors. There they began to build a new settlement, together. There they raised a flock of children, the blessing of their home. Today, as Mrs. Kytölä and her husband look back on their past life, they believe that God has been good to them. Only one of their children died, all others are living

It has not been just home, but outside the home as well, that Mrs. Kytölä has been much more than an average participant in common endeavors. She is a long-time member in the farmers' association, as well one of its most active members. At home, she has created handicrafts of great artistry, invariably winning prizes for them at local agricultural shows. I have learned all this from the residents of that area, concerning Mrs. Kytölä, always full of energy and bustle, that it can only reinforce the parallel to the worker ant: a workloving person finds the time and is capable of anything as long as there is a will and desire to give work its due respect.

I have always admired people who cannot boast of great riches, those who have earned their daily food and livelihood with their own hard work and industry, those who have raised many children to be decent people who follow in their mother and father's footsteps. It is a legacy that only a few people can leave as their inheritance. It is what the Kytöläs have achieved, and it is why I want to show Mrs. Kytölä as a paragon in all the chores and endeavors to which I accord respect and acknowledgement.

Some day in the future, when the Kytöläs grow old, as will happen, may Mrs. Kytölä pick up her pen again and leave the posterity another long story, to the admiration of the readers who will undoubtedly receive it with great pleasure. This writer is immensely delighted to express his gratitude to this youthful and respectable lady who still seems so youthful in her photograph, though we have learned that they will soon celebrate their 50th wedding anniversary. May God bless the members of such a family and home.

-- A. W. H.

Amalia's 50th anniversary